M. L. West is an Emeritus Fellow of All Souls College, Oxford, and a Fellow of the British Academy. From 1974 to 1991 he was Professor of Greek at Bedford and Royal Holloway Colleges, University of London. His many books include *The Orphic Poems* (1983), *An Introduction to Greek Metre* (1987), *Ancient Greek Music* (1992), *The East Face of Helicon* (1997) and *Indo-European Poetry and Myth* (2007).

'Translating the words and comprehending the meaning of Zoroaster's devotional poems is always challenging. M. L. West has produced a lucid interpretation of those ancient words. His renditions are filled with insights and empathy. This endeavour is an important contribution toward understanding more fully some of the earliest prophetic words in human history.'

Jamsheed K. Choksy, Professor of Iranian Studies, History, and India Studies, Indiana University

'A thoroughly worthwhile and refreshingly readable translation of the Older Avesta, M. L. West's book will be widely welcomed, by students and general readers alike.'

Almut Hintze, Zartoshty Reader in Zoroastrianism, School of Oriental and African Studies, London

'In this new and dauntless translation of the *Gāthās*, M. L. West resuscitates the notion of Zoroaster as the self-conscious founder of a new religion. In advancing this idea, he takes position against many modern interpreters of these extremely difficult texts. The clarity and beauty of his translation will be much welcomed by students of Zoroastrianism and by Zoroastrians themselves, while his bold interpretation will spark off welcome debate among specialists.'

Albert de Jong, Professor of Comparative Religion, Leiden University

The Hymns of Zoroaster

A New Translation of the Most Ancient Sacred Texts of Iran

With Introduction and Commentary by

M . L . West

BLOOMSBURY ACADEMIC

LONDON · NEW YORK · OXFORD · NEW DELHI · SYDNEY

BLOOMSBURY ACADEMIC
Bloomsbury Publishing Plc
50 Bedford Square, London, WC1B 3DP, UK
1385 Broadway, New York, NY 10018, USA
29 Earlsfort Terrace, Dublin 2, Ireland

BLOOMSBURY, BLOOMSBURY ACADEMIC and the Diana logo are
trademarks of Bloomsbury Publishing Plc

First published in 2010 by I.B. Tauris & Co Ltd
Reprinted by Bloomsbury Academic 2019 (twice), 2020 (twice), 2021, (twice), 2023

A catalogue record for this book is available from the British Library.

ISBN: PB: 978-1-3501-2746-3
eBook: 978-0-8577-3156-2
ePDF: 978-0-8577-1865-5

A catalog record for this book is available from the Library of Congress.

Typeset in Perpetua by Aptara Inc., New Delhi

To find out more about our authors and books visit
www.bloomsbury.com and sign up for our newsletters.

Contents

Preface

I became acquainted with the poems of Zoroaster some years ago while collecting materials for my *Indo-European Poetry and Myth* (Oxford 2007). I found that the available translations diverged considerably from one another, and that they all contained a good deal that seemed to me nonsense. I began to apply myself to study of the Old Avestan language in which the poems are written and, over time, to making a new translation for my own use. I soon became fascinated, not only with the problems of understanding the text, but with the personality and achievement of Zoroaster, a revolutionary religious thinker and leader who appeared from nowhere in a remote region of central Asia at the very dawn of Iranian history, or before it, and created a wonderful new faith that eventually became that of the entire Persian empire.

Here in these poems we have the very foundation texts of that religion and the authentic documentation of Zoroaster's own convictions and message. If they had been discovered last month, they would be a sensation. As it is, while the name of Zoroaster is vaguely familiar to many people, his poems are practically unknown. Zoroastrian priests have continued to recite them in the liturgy, but with very limited comprehension of the highly archaic language in which they are composed. For something over two centuries a small number of Western scholars have wrestled with them, achieving better understanding by degrees but generally focusing on linguistic details rather than on the sense of the whole, and debating among themselves rather than laying their results before a wider public in a digestible form. To a large extent they have been inhibited by their honest awareness of the many uncertainties of interpretation that still remain. At the same time the fact that the reading of these texts calls for specialist linguistic knowledge has meant that those who have engaged with them have usually been philologists who were more interested in the language than the content. Their translations have tended to be informed by a scrupulous concern for grammar and lexicography, unmoderated by a like concern for an intelligible and coherent train of thought.

In offering a new version I do not delude myself that all difficulties have been overcome and all obscurities resolved. I am conscious that many of them have not, so many indeed that if everything was not to be snowed under with question marks, only the most major uncertainties could be signalled as such. I believe nevertheless that by careful application I have succeeded more fully than my predecessors in penetrating to the sense of Zoroaster's utterances and in producing a translation that, besides being (and in consequence of being) more correct than any previous one, will be found more continuously intelligible, and hence more readable and more likely to impress the reader with the clarity and nobility of Zoroaster's religion. He was no purveyor of esoteric mumbo-jumbo but an outstanding figure in the world's intellectual history who fully deserves the attention of a modern public. The mists are thinning, and he can now be discerned in clearer outlines.

As an appendix to Zoroaster's own poems I have thought it appropriate to add the prose text that is the only other source for the earliest phase of Zoroastrianism: the *Liturgy in Seven Chapters*. This too is a wonderful document, at once a profession of faith and a structured series of prayers and praises that have all the freshness of a young religion and give the impression of ringing out somewhere in the middle of a fresh and hopeful young world.

M. L. West

Note on the pronunciation
of Avestan words and names

In the system of transcription used by modern Western scholars
letters have approximately the following values:

ą	a nasalized 'a', like French 'en'
å	as 'aw' in 'law'
aē	as 'y' in 'my'
ao	as 'ou' in 'loud'
β	like a 'w' pronounced through closed lips
c	as 'ch' in 'church'
δ	as 'th' in 'this'
ə	as 'a' in 'alone'
γ	as 'gh' in 'aargh' (on being strangled)
ii	as 'y' in 'yard'
ŋ	as 'ng' in 'sing'
ŋᵛ	the same combined with a 'w'
š	as 'sh' in 'ship'
θ	as 'th' in 'thing'
uu, v	as 'w' in 'twin'
x	as 'ch' in 'loch'
xᵛ	the same combined with a 'w'
ž	as 's' in 'pleasure'

A macron (as in ā, ē, etc.) indicates a lengthened vowel. Other
diacritics (as in ṇ, ń, ŋ́, ṣ, š́, ṭ, x́) may be ignored.

Introduction

Most people have come across the name of Zoroaster, and there may be many who think of him as some sort of ancient oriental sage or guru, of dubious repute as a fount of secret wisdom or knowledge. This is the image in which he has often been presented in Western literature, from the ancient Greeks to Nietzsche. But if one strips away the legends and falsifications and goes back to the genuine evidence, a different picture emerges. Zoroaster stands out in his true colours as one of the greatest and most radical religious reformers in the history of the world. The noble religion that he founded in Iran over 2,500 years ago is still practised to this day. The number of its adherents is small, perhaps about 130,000, most of them in western India (Gujarat and Mumbai), with some smaller communities in Iran and in other countries around the world.[1] But if Zoroastrianism can no longer count as one of the world's major faiths, it has the distinction of being one of the most ancient, much older than Christianity or Islam, older than Buddhism, older than anything one can properly call Judaism; only Hinduism can claim a greater antiquity. For

---

[1] The Indian Zoroastrians and their descendants in other lands are known as Parsis (or Parsees in the older English spelling).

more than a thousand years it was the official religion of a great empire.

Like other religions, it has evolved over time, and its founder's original system has not been preserved in its pure and simple form. It has undergone much elaboration and accommodation to other traditions. However, we are in the fortunate position of being able to read Zoroaster's message in his own words, in the poetic discourses with which he addressed his followers. They are not easy to understand, for reasons that will be explained. But the force of his intellect and the passion of his convictions speak to us across the millennia.

The sacred books of the Zoroastrians form an uneven collection known as the Avesta. They were composed at different dates, mainly before 300 BCE, in an Iranian language not otherwise documented and called by scholars Avestan. But what has been preserved is only a fraction of what once existed. The canonical Avesta, as it was edited and arranged under the Sasanian kings of Iran between the third and sixth centuries CE, consisted of 21 volumes. These were still current in the ninth century, and we have descriptions of their contents from Middle Persian sources of that time. But of this great body of writing only perhaps a quarter now remains, some of it in a fragmentary state.

The major components of the Avesta as it now exists, leaving aside various minor texts and fragments, are the *Yasna*, the *Yashts*, and the *Vīdēvdāt* or *Vendīdād*. The *Yasna* ('Worship') is a liturgical corpus, an assemblage of texts of different date recited by the priests in the divine service. The *Yashts* are hymns of praise, mostly metrical, addressed to various divinities and holy entities. The *Vīdēvdāt* ('Law against demons') is for the most part a sort of Zoroastrian Leviticus, a body of legal and ritual prescriptions.

2

The central core of the *Yasna* (chapters 28–53) consists of a series of more ancient texts. At their heart (chapters 35–41) sits the so-called *Liturgy (Yasna) in Seven Chapters*, a remarkable composition in hieratic prose created within the earliest Zoroastrian community not long after the prophet's lifetime. Enclosing it are the five *Gāthās* ('Songs'), which actually comprise seventeen separate poems, some 960 lines in all, arranged in five sequences according to metre. All the poems except the last (*Yasna* 53) were composed by Zoroaster himself.

These poems are the oldest texts in the Avesta and indeed the oldest in any Iranian language. Despite the many obscurities that hinder their interpetation, they are among the most precious legacies of antiquity. Philologists prize them as unique documents of an archaic Iranian tongue, of high value for the reconstruction of the common Indo-Iranian and Indo-European languages from which it was descended. They merit the attention of the wider public as the authentic utterances of an extraordinary religious leader whose thought was far ahead of his time. What would Christians not give for such a collection of religious poems by Jesus?

Zoroaster and his world

Certain modern scholars have maintained that Zoroaster was not the name of a historical but of a mythical personage, a mere construct. This view can only be called perverse. A single, distinct personality speaks to us out of the poems, and in several places the poet names himself as Zoroaster, or rather (in his own language) Zarathushtra. In the one poem that is not by him, *Yasna* 53, he is named again as a real person, either still living or of recent memory. In the later parts of the Avesta as well as in other Zoroastrian literature he is frequently spoken of, with never a doubt as to his historical reality. His existence is as well authenticated as that of most people in antiquity.

There is nothing lofty or spiritual about his name, which apparently meant 'Old-camel man'. He had the family surname Spitāma, which he shared with some other persons mentioned in the poems. We cannot pinpoint the region of Iran where the Spitāmas lived, but it certainly lay somewhere in the eastern territories that included modern Afghanistan and parts of Turkmenistan, Uzbekistan, Tajikistan, and Pakistan. This was the homeland of the Avesta as a whole. The geographical references that occur in it all relate to these eastern lands,[2] and its language differs considerably from what we call Old Persian, which was the language of the south-west (Persia proper, the seat of the Achaemenid kings, the modern province of Fars). Not that the language of the Avesta is uniform: the *Gāthās* and the *Seven Chapters* are in a different dialect from the rest – more archaic, but the differences are not all accounted for by development over time – and Zoroaster must have lived in a different area from those where the later Avestan texts took shape. According to a Zoroastrian tradition that may go back to one of the lost books of the Avesta, he came from a district called Ragha, apparently to be located in Badakhshan in the north-eastern corner of Afghanistan, or in ancient terms eastern Bactria.[3]

As to when he lived, scholars are divided between those who put him in the seventh or sixth century BCE and those who uphold

---

[2] See Gherardo Gnoli, *Zoroaster's Time and Homeland*, 129–58; Frantz Grenet in V. S. Curtis and Sarah Stewart (eds.), *Birth of the Persian Empire* (London 2005), 29–51.

[3] See F. Grenet (as previous note), 36–8. Some Greek authors too, perhaps beginning with the historian Ctesias about 400 BCE, located Zoroaster in Bactria. Diodorus Siculus (1. 94. 2) follows some earlier writer who had placed 'Zathraustes' among the Ariaspai, that is, in Seistan. Later Zoroastrian tradition put the prophet's home in north-western Iran, but this will reflect spurious claims made after the religion had established itself in those parts.

a much higher dating, around 1000 BCE or even earlier. The latter party take their stand on the fact that the language of the *Gāthās* is approximately as archaic as the related Indian dialect in which the hymns of the Rigveda are composed; these are themselves not closely dated but are conventionally assigned to the period 1500–1000. (1200–900 might be more realistic.) But the argument is not at all reliable, as an archaic form of speech may maintain itself for centuries with little change in an out-of-the-way region such as Zoroaster's homeland may have been. One cannot take a body of texts in an otherwise undocumented language and declare on linguistic grounds that they must belong to the second and not the first millennium BCE. On general grounds it seems unlikely that Zoroaster should be separated from the rest of Iranian history by such a wide time gap.

The latest possible date for his activity is the mid sixth century BCE, as the religion he created, defined by the worship of Ahura Mazdā instead of the traditional Indo-Iranian deities, is that of the Achaemenid kings of Persia from the time of Darius I, who ruled from 522 to 486. Mary Boyce has argued that it was also the religion of Darius' royal predecessors Cyrus and Cambyses, but this is questionable.[4] It may have been Darius' family religion, as his father Vishtāspa (the Hystaspes of Greek authors) had the same name as a figure famous in Zoroastrian tradition, the Vishtaaspa whom the prophet himself names as his principal champion. There are four possible explanations for this: that the two men were the same; that Darius' father was a later member of the same family as Zoroaster's patron; that he was of an unrelated family but named after the Zoroastrian; or that the coincidence of names was purely fortuitous. The first

---

4 Mary Boyce, *A History of Zoroastrianism*, ii. 41–3, 49–69, and in *Achaemenid History* iii (Proceedings of the London Achaemenid History Workshop, Leiden 1988), 26–31.

cannot be right, as the authors of the later Avesta who celebrated Vishtaaspa's crusading battles could not possibly have ignored it if his son had become master of the Persian empire. And if he had been a forebear of Darius' father, Darius would have known it and would have included him in the line of his ancestors that he records in his great inscription at Bisitun. On the other hand, it might seem too much of a coincidence if a Zoroastrian king's father happened to be called Vishtāspa without reference to Zoroaster's famous patron. The inference is that Vishtāspa's father Arshāma (Arsames), who presumably bestowed that name on him, was already a Zoroastrian.

How much earlier are we to place Zoroaster? The Avesta itself, or what we have of it, gives no chronological indications or historical anchorage. However, in a lost book of the Avesta, cited by the tenth-century Arabic writer Mascūdī, Zoroaster was represented as having prophesied that the empire would be destroyed after three hundred years but that the religion would last for a thousand. This underlies a chronological scheme reflected in other Arabic and Pahlavi sources, according to which Zoroaster was born, or attained enlightenment, three hundred years before the conquest of Iran by Alexander the Great (330 BCE). The prophecy must have been invented, shortly after Alexander's conquest, by some Zoroastrian who was dismayed by the fall of the Achaemenid empire but fortified himself with the confidence that the religion would continue for centuries into the future. He evidently thought of the prophet as having lived a century before the accession of Darius, around the time of the end of the Assyrian empire and the rise of the Median. We do not know the basis for this reckoning – there is no historical plausibility in the notion of some scholars that from the time of the prophet the Zoroastrian priests had carefully kept a tally of the passing years – but it yields a dating that sits well with the rest of our evidence and may not be far wrong.

It receives some support from another line of argument. Already in the fifth century (if not the sixth) Zoroastrian theologians had constructed a chronological scheme according to which the struggle between the good and evil principles, Ahura Mazdā and Angra Manyu, was being played out over a period of twelve thousand years, divided into four equal parts. At the end of the first three thousand years the material world was created, together with all people's *fravashis* or external souls. After another six thousand years Zoroaster's good religion won acceptance.[5] In the remaining three thousand years Angra Manyu will be finally defeated, and thereafter everything will remain perfect and unchanging. Zoroaster then, in this scheme, appears at the start of the tenth millennium of the world. The creator of the system almost certainly considered himself and his contemporaries to be living in that same millennium, and not more than half way through it. Such is the viewpoint reflected in a late Jewish text, 4 Ezra (2 Esdras) 14. 10–12, probably written around 100 CE:

> For the world has lost its youth, the times begin to wax old. For the world age is divided into twelve parts; nine (parts) of it are passed already, and the half of the tenth part; and there remain of it two (parts), besides the half of the tenth part.

This must derive directly or indirectly from a Zoroastrian source, no doubt of post-Alexandrian date, in which Zoroaster was conceived to have lived about half a millennium previously.

---

[5] The earliest clear evidence for this scheme is a report by the Greek historian Theopompus, writing in the fourth century BCE, but it must have been established for some time before that. It is set out in detail in Middle Persian sources.

Classical Greek writers who refer to Zoroaster put him at various dates and clearly had no solid information. Some authors of the fifth and fourth centuries BCE had the idea that he had lived six thousand years before.[6] This is an impossibly early dating, but we can see where it must have come from: from a misunderstanding of that Zoroastrian chronology, in which the prophet's soul was created at the end of the first trimillennium, six thousand years before his birth. Other Greeks thought of him as having lived much later, long after the Trojan War. Aristotle's pupil Aristoxenus represented him as having given instruction to Pythagoras in Babylon, sometime in the early or mid sixth century; this was a fiction of Aristoxenus', who was not bound by any great historical scruples, but he must have thought of Zoroaster as a figure from the time of the Median empire. Others put him a couple of centuries earlier, in the time of the legendary Assyrian king Ninos and queen Semiramis. This is part of a novelistic, pseudo-historical construction in which the Assyrians invade Bactria, where Zoroaster is king at the time.

The society reflected in the *Gāthās* is loosely structured. There is no sense of a central imperial authority. Zoroaster speaks in several places of a hierarchy of social units, starting with the *xᵛaētu-* (family, clan) and rising to the *vərəzəna-* (local community) and *aryaman-* (a wider network or alliance, perhaps something like a tribe).[7] He has a separate scale for the domains within which personal authority (*xšaϑra-*) may be exercised, from the individual household (*dəmāna-*) through the *vīs-* (manor) to the *šōiϑra-* (settlement) and the *dax́yu-* (region).[8] The last corresponds to

---

[6] Xanthus of Sardis, Eudoxus, Aristotle, and others; see A. V. Williams Jackson, *Zoroaster. The Prophet of Ancient Iran*, 152–4.

[7] *Yasna* 32. 1; 33. 3–4; 46. 1; 49. 7. Cf. Paul Thieme, *Mitra and Aryaman* (New Haven 1957), 80. – For the pronunciation of Avestan words see p. xi.

[8] *Yasna* 31. 16, 18; 46. 4; 48. 10, 12; 53. 8.

the word later used by Darius and his successors for the provinces into which their empire was divided. It is the largest political unit in Zoroaster's world. He speaks critically of the 'rulers of the region' or 'of the regions'.⁹ But they appear as rather dim and distant figures.

It is a pastoral society in which the cow and its products have an important place. But the dairy-farmer's peaceful existence is threatened by violent intrusions. In one of his most striking poems (*Yasna* 29) Zoroaster represents the cow's soul as complaining to the powers above of the cruel aggression to which she is subject. It is not her righteous-living herdsman that is to blame, but others who, guided by priests of a false religion, drive her off and condemn her to be sacrificed.¹⁰

This is the most specific of the ills in his society that Zoroaster condemns and would like to cure. If he cannot achieve this, it is because he lacks temporal power; he has not got the wealth and influence and the numbers of supporters that would enable him to change things.¹¹ There is thus a political element in his aspirations. He hopes to convert people to the true way by the persuasive force of his message. At the same time he dreams of a power centre from which he could impose what he sees as the divine will. In the end he seems to have had some success, finding a strong patron in Vishtaaspa and establishing a community of the faithful large enough to endure and prosper.

Zoroaster's religion

What was the new religion that he preached? First we must try to form a concept of the older religion that he aimed to supplant.

---

⁹ *Yasna* 46. 1; 48. 10.
¹⁰ See also *Yasna* 31. 9–10; 32. 8, 10, 12, 14; 33. 4; 44. 6, 20; 51. 14.
¹¹ *Yasna* 29. 9–10; 46. 2.

The evidence for it is largely indirect. Besides hints in the *Gāthās*, it is a matter of inference from the related culture of Vedic India and from fragmented survivals in later Iran.

The picture is of a traditional polytheism inherited from the time of common Indo-Iranian culture in the earlier second millennium BCE. Some of the same gods appear in both Iran and India. One of the more prominent Vedic deities, Mitra the god of contracts, was also worshipped in Iran (as Mithra) and is the subject of a major hymn in the Avesta (*Yasht* 10). In other *Yashts* there are references to the wind god Vayu and to the mysterious deity known as the Grandson of the Waters; these too are familiar from the Rigveda. Two further Vedic divinities, Aryaman and Narāśaṃsa, appear elsewhere in the Avesta as objects of reverence. Others again such as Indra, Nāsatya, and Śarva are named in the *Vīdēvdāt* as demons, evidently still respected in parts of Iran but rejected by pious Zoroastrians.

Some forms of worship too were common to both countries. The sacral fire had an honoured place in cult in both, and so did the exhilarating drink made from the pressed-out juice (Vedic *soma-*, Avestan *haoma-*) of a certain mountain plant. There were cultic personnel in both countries with similar titles: the fire-priest (*atharvan-*, *āϑravan-*), the libation-priest (*hotar-*, *zaotar-*), the eulogist (*stotar-*, *staotar-*), and the poet-seer (*r̥ṣi-*, *ərəši-*). In the cults of both countries the cow was highly esteemed, and importance was attached in both to the holy utterance (*mantra-*, *mąϑra-*).

The traditional gods were known in India as *devas*, from an ancient Indo-European word **deiwos* meaning 'celestial one'. Another honorific title, applied in India to a secondary group of deities, was *asura-*, 'lord'. Both terms were current in pre-Zoroastrian Iran too, where they appeared respectively as *daiva-* (in Avestan *daēva-*) and *ahura-*. Zoroaster promoted a new set of beings as the proper object of worship. It was not appropriate to call them *daēvas*, as they did not belong to the traditional pantheon of 'celestials'. So he classified them as *ahuras* and, with the bold decisiveness of the true revolutionary, relegated the entire category of *daēvas* to the status of demons unworthy of worship.

Chief among his Lords was Ahura Mazdā, the Lord who takes thought or pays attention, or as I have chosen to render him, the Mindful Lord.[12] This is a deity identified not by an opaque conventional name, like the old gods, but by reference to his essential quality of attentiveness or intelligence. His intelligence is creative and supervisory. He created this world, or at any rate what is good in it, by means of his thought.[13] He observes men's moral deliberations and choices with a watchful eye, and he cannot be deceived.[14] He communicates his wisdom through visions and utterances that Zoroaster receives; men are his messengers.[15]

Zoroaster addresses Ahura Mazdā constantly throughout his poems. In addressing him, however, he very often uses pronouns and verbs in the second person plural, as I have made clear in the translation by distinguishing scrupulously between Thou and Ye.

[12] Zoroaster often refers to him simply as Mazdā, 'the Mindful one', or as Ahura, 'the Lord'. When he uses both terms together, he does not have them in a fixed order, and they can be separated by other words. In later Zoroastrianism Ahura Mazdā became a fixed combination, appearing in the Achaemenid royal inscriptions as Auramazdā and in Middle Persian as Ohrmazd.

[13] *Yasna* 31. 7, 11; 51. 16; cf. 54. 1.

[14] *Yasna* 31. 13; 43. 6; 45. 4. The concept of an all-seeing god with a celestial eye, or many eyes, not to be deceived, was taken over from the traditional religion. In the Rigveda these are the characteristics of Varuna or Mitra–Varuna, and they remain attached to Mithra in the Avestan hymn to him (*Yasht* 10). The eye was sometimes identified with the sun. See my *Indo-European Poetry and Myth* (Oxford 2007), 171–2, 198–9.

[15] *Yasna* 28. 6, 11; 31. 3, 8; 32. 1; 43. 5, 11; 45. 3, 5. Mazdā is the source of 'mantras', that is, pieces of instruction to be learned and repeated: 28. 7; 29. 7; 43. 14; 44. 14; 45. 3. I have translated the word as 'prescript', though of course no writing was involved.

These plurals are not merely honorific. Their reference is made plain by two passages where the prophet speaks of 'Mazdā and Ahuras', in other words 'Mazdā and the other Lords'.[16] Mazdā, then, is the leader of a concordant group, and it is a matter of indifference whether one addresses them collectively or Mazdā individually.

Zoroaster nowhere identifies the other Ahuras explicitly, but we can assume that he is thinking of certain divine entities which he constantly associates with Mazdā and sometimes addresses in the vocative. Their names are the names of abstract qualities, mostly of an ethical nature: Right (*Aša*); Good Thought (*Vohu manah*); Piety (*Ārmati*); Bounteous Will (*Spənta manyu*); Dominion (*Xšaϑra*). These are all things that human beings may have in themselves, and Zoroaster often uses the words with reference to his own or other people's thinking and conduct, besides treating them as personified beings with an independent existence. Sometimes it is not clear which way to take them, and whether to translate them with a capital or a lower-case initial. When they are personified they can be treated like the conventional gods of poetry and represented as speaking to one another or to mankind.[17]

Right had long been recognized in Indo-Iranian religion as a cosmic power. The Avestan *Aša* is etymologically identical with the Vedic *R̥ta*, a divine principle that governs the natural world, for example the course of the sun, as well as representing truth or rightness in the human sphere. Zoroaster made it the defining principle of his religion. The antithesis of Right and Wrong encapsulates the whole of his moral concern. The human race is divided between the *ašavans*, the possessors or followers of

[16] *Yasna* 30. 9; 31. 4; cf. 28. 1, 'You all'.
[17] *Yasna* 29. 2–4; 44. 8; 45. 2; 46. 9.

Right, and the *drəgvants*, those who belong to Wrong. But Aṣa is subordinated to Ahura Mazdā, who is called his father.[18]

Mazdā is likewise the father of Good Thought (also called Best Thought).[19] This is what people are urged to cultivate above all else. Often it is coupled with good speech and good action; Zoroaster was so far as we know the first to formulate the triad 'thought, word, and deed'. Good Thought is the one most emphasized, as it is the foundation for the other two. Zoroaster sometimes speaks of Good Thought's own utterances or actions (enactments). Its opposite, Bad or Worst Thought, is also mentioned, but not as a divine power that people might invoke.

Zoroaster's emphasis on mental attitude and moral deliberation also finds expression in the figures of Piety (Ārmati) and Bounteous Will. Ārmati corresponds to Vedic *aramati-* and means something like appropriate thinking, rightmindedness, devotion to what is good or holy. Spənta Manyu, the Bounteous or Liberal or Positive Will, has a twin brother who is his opposite: Angra Manyu, the Hostile or Negative Will. Zoroaster sets out his doctrine of the two Wills most explicitly in *Yasna* 30. He describes how they tussle for a man's soul, making their voices heard in his mind, and how his choice between them determines his ultimate fate. In another passage about inner voices it is Piety who debates with the man's will as he ponders his options.[20] The doctrinal variant is of no significance, as the basic idea is the same. The epithet *spənta-* (related to Russian *svyatoy* 'holy, saintly') is often applied to Piety herself, as well as to Ahura Mazdā and to the man who is bounteous or liberal in his actions. The Bounteous

---

[18] *Yasna* 47. 2, cf. 44. 3. I say 'his' because although *aṣa-* is a neuter noun (nominative *aṣəm*), in a few places where it is personified Zoroaster uses a nominative and vocative of animate gender, *aṣā*, probably intending it as a masculine. See *Iran* 44 (2007), 77.

[19] *Yasna* 31. 8; 45. 4.

[20] *Yasna* 31. 11–13. See also 43. 16; 45. 2; 47. 1–6.

Will is also a feature of Ahura Mazdā, since his whole order is good and a manifestation of his liberal or bounteous nature. He is praised as the father of this Will, as he is elsewhere of Right and Good Thought.[21]

Dominion (Xšaθra) is again a property of Ahura Mazdā as well as being something that humans aspire to. Mazdā's dominion, however, is not total and absolute. It is represented as something that mankind must fight to promote. It is strengthened, and he is increased, when they follow Piety and Good Thought.[22] It is a striking feature of Zoroaster's religion that his Ahuras and their antagonists the Daēvas do not live in a separate world and are not self-sufficient. They operate on earth through their human adherents, and the extent of their power and authority depends on their success in getting people to listen to them.

Besides the various personifications, Right, Good Thought, and the rest, certain other divine figures with self-explanatory names are mentioned here and there in the *Gāthās*: the Maker of the Cow; the Shaper (of everything); the Creator of Wrong. These designations avoid giving specific answers to the questions of *who* made the cow or created Wrong (though in other passages Zoroaster is prepared to identify the cow's maker as Ahura Mazdā or the Bounteous Will).[23] When the prophet declares at the end of *Yasna* 51, 'those (immortals) who have been and are, I will worship under their own names', he means that he uses names

---

[21] *Yasna* 47. 3. As in another poem (30. 3) the good and bad Wills are called twins, it ought to follow that Ahura Mazdā was also the father of the bad one. But Zoroaster never intended this conclusion, and it was left to later Zoroastrians to draw it and wrestle with it.

[22] *Yasna* 28. 3; 30. 8; 31. 7; 33. 10, 12; 34. 1, 11; 44. 6; 46. 16.

[23] The Maker of the Cow: 29. 2; 31. 9; 46. 9; identified with Ahura Mazdā, 44. 6, 51. 7; with the Bounteous Will, 47. 3. The Shaper: 29. 6. (He seems to be a traditional figure, as the Avestan θβōrəštar corresponds to the Vedic creator Tvaṣṭṛ.) The Creator of Wrong: 51. 10.

that correspond to the reality of the divinity in question instead
of the old mythological names that mostly conveyed no meaning
and appeared to be arbitrary.

Zoroaster's new religion calls for active struggle on the part
of humankind. If the world that Mazdā created in the beginning
had been preserved intact, all would be well. But it has become
corrupted through the actions of followers of Wrong, such as the
mythical Yima who first slaughtered the cow and portioned out
its meat for human consumption.[24] Such people are 'destroyers
of this existence'.[25] We must strive to restore the perfection of
the First Existence, the world as it was originally. Perhaps this
can be achieved in our lifetime, perhaps it will take longer. 'May
we be the ones who will make this world splendid.'[26] The fol-
lower of Right who contributes towards this goal is awarded the
honourable title of *ahūmbiš-*, 'healer of the world', or *saošyant-*,
'(would-be) strengthener, enhancer, fosterer, promoter' (of the
religion, and so of Mazdā's dominion).[27]

Zoroaster is not interested only in moral welfare; he also
wants physical well-being to go with it. Among the things that he
represents Ahura Mazdā as having at his disposal and dispensing to
those who deserve it there appears repeatedly the pair *haurvatāt-*
and *amərətatāt-*, often misleadingly translated as 'wholeness and
immortality'. 'Wholeness' is literally correct, but it refers to
haleness of body, good health and freedom from sickness. As for
amərətatāt-, while it corresponds etymologically to *immort(ali)ty*,
it means literally 'not dying', and what Zoroaster is hoping for is
not eternal life but continuing life, that is, not to die before his

[24] *Yasna* 32. 8.
[25] *Yasna* 32. 13. Cf. 46. 11; 53. 6.
[26] *Yasna* 30. 9. Cf. 28. 11; 33. 1; 34. 15; 44. 2; 50. 11.
[27] *Yasna* 31. 19; 44. 2, 16; 34. 13; 45. 11; 46. 3; 48. 9, 12; 53. 2.

time. It is a boon for this world, not the next. In other passages he speaks of 'long life'.[28]

He does have a doctrine about continuing existence after death, but it is not formulated in terms of 'eternal life'. Like many another religious leader, he reinforces his moral message by giving notice of contrasting fates awaiting the good and the wicked. The soul of the departed will arrive, with a clear or a troubled conscience, at a narrow bridge or causeway, the Arbiter's Crossing.[29] There he must make his declaration to Ahura Mazdā, who will decide his fate by means of an ordeal involving fire and molten metal.[30] This is the 'Supplication' or 'Reckoning'.[31] The righteous will dwell with Ahura Mazdā and Good Thought in a place of joy and radiance,[32] whereas those found unworthy will endure aeons of darkness and woe, with only foul food to eat.[33]

The alternatives of light and darkness seem again to echo a traditional concept.[34] At the same time the radiant brightness promised to the good corresponds to an intrinsic feature of Ahura Mazdā's realm. Zoroaster associates the activities of Right and Good Thought with the daylight and the sun. They are 'the

---

[28] *Yasna* 33. 5; 43. 2, 13.

[29] *Yasna* 46. 10–11; 51. 13. The bridge leading to the land of the dead was a traditional element of popular mythology, perhaps Indo-European; see my *Indo-European Poetry and Myth*, 390.

[30] *Yasna* 30. 2; 31. 3, 19; 32. 7; 34. 4; 43. 4, 9; 46. 7; 47. 6; 51. 9. Ancient India and Greece both knew the custom by which someone suspected of wrongdoing could undertake to prove his or her innocence by walking unscathed through fire or by contact with red-hot or molten metal.

[31] *Yasna* 30. 2; 49. 9; 31. 14.

[32] *Yasna* 31. 20, 22; 46. 14; 48. 7.

[33] *Yasna* 31. 20; cf. 30. 4, 11.

[34] Cf. Rigveda 2. 27. 14, 'may I attain the broad, safe Light, Indra; may the long Darkness not overtake us'.

gladness beheld by the daylight', 'these amenities permeating the world of light'. Right itself is 'sunlit', whereas

> That is the man who perverts good repute, who declares that the worst thing to behold
> with the eyes is the cow, and the sun.[35]

Frashaushtra, one of Zoroaster's friends, is said to 'expose his body to the Good Religion', as if to the sunlight (51. 17).

There is an impressive clarity and simplicity in Zoroaster's religion as it appears in the *Gāthās*. It is not cluttered up with mystical or theological baggage. Its pantheon is not made up of assorted characters from an obscure prehistoric mythology but of beings with clearly defined identities and properties. Its ethics is plain and straightforward. It is concerned not with irrational rules and taboos but with easily understood moral and intellectual values. The emphasis is on divine and human sapience and on man's responsibility for the choices he makes between good and bad.

Zoroaster as poet and preacher

As the self-conscious creator of a new faith – 'the religion of mine that I am to perfect' (44. 9) – Zoroaster was free to define his own role and status in it. He invented no novel title for himself but drew on the existing language of cult. He calls himself a *zaotar-* or minister, and a *rishi* or poet-prophet; he is Ahura Mazdā's 'praiser', and his 'mantra-man', that is, the one who receives and

---

35 *Yasna* 30. 1; 31. 7; 32. 2, cf. 53. 4; 32. 10. The last passage may allude to sacrificial rites performed at night. Cf. also 50. 2, 10; *Seven Chapters*, 37. 4.

passes on his prescripts.[36] These are loosely descriptive terms, not formal positions in a church. Zoroaster does not represent himself as officiating at ritual activities. Although he sometimes uses the language of liturgy, speaking of praying 'with outstretched hands' or of making dedications and offerings, this all seems to be meant figuratively, not literally.[37] In several places he refers to a *maga-*, or great *maga-*, a word that appears to signify some kind of sacramental event, but again it is not clear that a specific ritual is in question. It seems in some cases to be something that is being prepared for rather than already in progress.[38]

If the *Gāthās* were not performed at a ritual, what was their intended function? Under what conditions were they heard? For all the innumerable addresses to Mazdā and other Ahuras, these are not private devotions that Zoroaster uttered in solitude to his gods. He meant them for a human audience. Nor is he fulminating at a hostile crowd of unbelievers and sceptics. In a number of poems he addresses his followers, whom he characterizes as *išəntō*, people eager to come from near and from far.[39] He speaks of coming before them to proclaim his gospel; 'facing the zealous I will be heard in the house of song.'[40] They are the people he refers to as his 'supporters' (28. 2) and as 'the men of Observance' (48. 10, if rightly interpreted).

In other passages he addresses individuals, some of whom are of his own Spitāma family. At 46. 15 it is the Haecataspa Spitāmas; the two sons of Hugava to whom he turns in the following stanzas,

---

[36] *zaotar-, Yasna* 33. 6; *ərəši-*, 31. 5; *staotar-*, 50. 11, cf. 30. 1, 34. 15, 45. 8, 49. 12; *maθran-*, 32. 13, 50. 5–6.

[37] See *Yasna* 28. 1; 29. 5; 33. 7, 14; 34. 1–3; 50. 8–9.

[38] *Yasna* 29. 11; 46. 14; 51. 16; 53. 7; persons involved with it (*magavans*), 51. 15. (At 33. 7 the word apparently refers to conventional cult practitioners.)

[39] *Yasna* 30. 1; 45. 1; cf. 31. 18; 47. 6. In the translation I have used 'proselytes'.

[40] *Yasna* 31. 2; 50. 4. In the later Avesta 'the house of song' becomes a term for Paradise, but in the *Gāthās* it evidently means the place where Zoroaster delivers his poetic addresses to his followers.

Frashaushtra and Djāmaaspa, were perhaps allied by marriage. At 51. 16–19 they appear again beside Madyaimāha Spitāma and the Kavi Vishtaaspa, Zoroaster's patron.[41]

What I am calling for convenience Zoroaster's 'hymns', then, may be characterized as songs or poems that he sang or recited at gatherings of his family and/or his followers, and in which he voiced his devotional and other aspirations. Some of the gatherings may have been intimate, others larger; at 34. 1 he speaks of 'us in our great numbers', and even if he is including absent with present supporters, it seems likely that there were occasions when all of them who were able came together to hear their leader's poetic discourses.

The poems are cast in what were no doubt traditional metrical forms, showing a distant affinity to those of the Rigveda. They are all composed in stanzas of three, four, or five lines. Each stanza is usually self-contained in sense, but occasionally a complex statement is spread across two or more. In the three-line stanzas quite often the first two lines make up one sentence and the third another. Each line is divided by a caesura into two members or cola (or in *Yasna* 53 three), and in each colon the number of syllables is more or less fixed.

At a more ancient stage of Iranian versification there had probably been some regular scheme governing the placing of long and short syllables, especially at the end of each line, as in the Vedic hymns, but in the *Gāthās* it is hard to detect anything

---

[41] Frasha-ushtra's name contains the same 'camel' element as Zarath-ushtra. For him see also 28. 8; 49. 8; 53. 2; plural Djāmaaspas in 49. 9. In the one Gāthic poem that is not Zoroaster's own work (53. 2) Vishtaaspa is himself designated as a Spitāma, and indeed as *Zaraθuštriš*, which could mean 'Zoroaster's son' but is more probably to be understood as 'Zoroaster's follower', 'Zoroastrian'. In the next stanza the poet addresses 'Porucistā of the Haecataspa Spitāmas, youngest of Zoroaster's daughters'. These may be actual daughters of Zoroaster's or just his female followers. It is noteworthy that men and women appear to enjoy equal status in the cult, cf. *Yasna* 46. 10; 54. 1; and in the *Seven Chapters*, 35. 6; 37. 3; 39. 2; 41. 2.

of the kind. All we can say is that there is a strong tendency for words of three or more syllables to be put at the end of a colon.

In the *Yasna* the poems appear arranged in five sequences (the five *Gāthās*) according to the stanza-form used in each:

Yasna 28–34: three lines, each of 7 + 9 syllables.
Yasna 43–46: five lines, each of 4 + 7 syllables.
Yasna 47–50: four lines, each of 4 + 7 syllables.
Yasna 51: three lines, each of 7 + 7 syllables.
Yasna 53: four lines, two of 7 + 5 and two of 7 + 7 + 5 syllables.

We cannot assume that this arrangement goes back to Zoroaster himself or that it corresponds to the order of composition. It is true that the first poem appears to begin programmatically, anticipating some of the main themes of other poems, and that in two cases (*Yasna* 31 and 48) a poem seems to start from where the previous one ended. But elsewhere poems that belong together thematically are more widely separated, and we cannot follow a continuous thread of development.

The diction of the hymns contains traditional elements, as is evident from the fact that some expressions have Vedic parallels. Zoroaster's general tone is lofty, but he does not always avoid direct and earthy expressions when he wants to condemn something. He resorts readily to personification. We have seen that entities such as Good Thought and Piety are important in his theology, but other personified abstracts that appear in single contexts seem to be momentary creations of poetic style rather than of settled religious doctrine: Contempt, Compliance, Reward, Silent Meditation, Good Dispensation.[42]

It throws an interesting sidelight on Zoroaster's society that he several times draws imagery from the racecourse or from

[42] *Yasna* 32. 3; 43. 12, 15; 49. 1.

speeding horses.[43] His commonest images, however, are those of the house and the path. He speaks of the house of Good Thought, the house of Worst Thought, the house of Wrong, the house of Ahura Mazdā, and the house of song;[44] of the path or paths of Good Thought, of enhancement, of enlightenment, of enablement, of the religion itself; of the path for the soul to follow.[45] Another image that reflects his standing concerns is that of the 'pasture of Right and Good Thought' (33. 3).

The Seven Chapters

The *Liturgy in Seven Chapters* is in the same archaic form of Avestan as the *Gāthās* and must have been composed not very long afterwards, though probably after Zoroaster's death. It is a text to be spoken by a priest before a congregation of worshippers. He speaks as their representative and on their behalf. The sacred fire is burning on the altar, and libations are being made.

The style is formal and elevated, the structure carefully shaped. The first chapter is an affirmation of what the Zoroastrians stand for and of their commitment to Ahura Mazdā and Right. In the second chapter the sacred fire is invoked as a manifestation of Mazdā and his Bounteous Will. His praises are developed in the third chapter, with reference to his creation of the earth, the waters, the plants, and all things good. From here the scope widens: the earth and the waters themselves receive praises and

---

[43] See *Yasna* 29. 8; 30. 10; 43. 5–6; 44. 4; 48. 2; 49. 9; 50. 6, 7; 51. 6. 'Horse' (*aspa-*) appears as an element in the names Vishta-aspa, Djāma-aspa, and Haecat-aspa. According to the later Avesta Zoroaster himself was the son of Porušaspa, 'Greyhorse'.

[44] *Yasna* 30. 10, 32. 15, 44. 9; 32. 13; 46. 6, 11, 49. 11, 51. 14; 49. 10; 45. 8, 50. 4, 51. 15.

[45] *Yasna* 33. 5, 34. 12–13, 51. 16; 43. 3; 46. 4; 50. 4; 53. 2; 44. 8.

worship, followed by the Cow's soul (canonized by Zoroaster in *Yasna* 29) and all other righteous souls, human or animal. When all the objects of worship have been named and summed up in a general formula, the focus comes back to Ahura Mazdā, and in the two last chapters a series of prayers is addressed to him, with pointed allusions to the offerings being made.

It is a marvellously sunny text: there is no reference to any difficulties faced by the community, and only the slightest hint of anything or anyone bad in the world. This is one thing that differentiates it from the *Gāthās*. Another is the extension of worship beyond Zoroaster's Ahuras to the earth, the waters, and the entire horde of the souls of the righteous.

What we are seeing here are developments shaped by two factors: on the one hand the acceptance of some elements of traditional popular religion into Zoroastrian cult, and on the other the impulse to integrate and justify them. People had long worshipped the earth and the waters; here they are worshipped as parts of Mazdā's creation, the female spirits who inhabit the earth are turned into personifications of aspects of Zoroastrian cult,[46] and the waters become 'the Lord's wives'. People had long invoked the souls of the ancestors; here the concept of the good souls of former mortals, which still have power to confer benefit, is expanded to take in the souls of those still living and those yet to be born, all the righteous ones, that is, together with the famous Cow's soul from the *Gāthās*.

Three detached mantras

At the end of chapter 27 of the *Yasna*, just before the *Gāthās*, there appear three independent stanzas, unconnected with one

---

[46] See the note on the fourth chapter (*Yasna* 38. 1–2).

another, that are clearly of early date. They are revered by Zoroastrians as sacred mantras and have been placed where they are for that reason. The first may well go back to Zoroaster himself: it is in the same metrical form as the seven poems of *Yasna* 28–34, and its thought and language are in complete accord with those of the *Gāthās*. It may perhaps be a stanza detached from one of the longer poems (though there is no obvious place where it fits), or it may be all that remains of a poem otherwise lost. I render it as follows (27. 13):

> Even as he is the master one would choose, so the direction in
>   line with Right
> and Good Thought of the world's actions is assigned to the
>   Mindful One,
> and the dominion, to the Lord whom they give to the poor as
>   pastor.

The second is couched in equally pure archaic language, but the metrical form (4 + 5, 4 + 4, 3 + 5 syllables) does not accord with any of the *Gāthās*, and the rather sophisticated idea expressed, that Right sets its own standard of Right, is not one that Zoroaster himself voices, though he would surely not have contested it. It may have been composed by one of his early disciples. There are ambiguities in the syntax and various interpretations are possible. Mine is (27. 14):

> Right is good, it is the best;
> ideal it is, ideal to itself,
> whatever best Right sees as Right.

The third is a little less archaic in its linguistic form, and the metrical structure is again uncanonical (5 + 7 + 7, 4 + 4, 4 + 4). It clumsily adapts a stanza of Zoroaster's, perhaps misconstruing it in taking 'the Mindful Lord' as the subject of 'knows' (51. 22), while the naming of both male and female entities as objects of worship echoes the *Seven Chapters* (39. 2–3). It runs (27. 15):

> That one of the Beings in whose worship the Mindful Lord
>   knows is the better (interest)
> in accord with Right, and of the female ones,
> those males and those females we worship.

Subsequent developments

As was noted earlier, Zoroaster complains more than once of his weakness and lack of political power. At one point he is alienated from his surroundings and wondering where he can escape:

> What land for refuge, where am I to go for refuge?
> They set me apart from clan and tribe;
> I am not pleased with the communities I consort with,
> nor with the region's wrongful rulers.
> How am I to please Thee, Mindful Lord? (46. 1)

He knows that if his religion is to take root he needs to find someone of influence who will take it up and promote it.

> This I ask Thee, tell me straight, Lord:
> the religion of mine that I am to perfect,
> how might the master of a beneficent dominion proclaim it
>   for me
> with righteous rule, a very potent follower of Thine, Mindful
>   One,
> abiding with Right and Good Thought? . . .
>
> How might piety spread to those
> to whom Thy religion, Mindful One, goes forth? (44. 9, 11)

He found the patron he sought in the Kavi Vishtaaspa, who as we have seen may have been a relative. The title *kavi-* means something like 'seer, poet'. In two passages (32. 14–15, 46. 11) Zoroaster speaks critically of the Kavis as a class associated with the Karpans (a kind of priest); but he implies that they have been led astray by the followers of Wrong rather than being intrinsically evil. Vishtaaspa at any rate is exempt from his strictures. He is acclaimed as a righteous man and as Zoroaster's 'ally for the great *maga-*' (46. 14).

> That insight the Kavi Vishtaaspa, with his control of the *maga-*, attained
> by the paths of Good Thought, the one which he meditated with Right,
> to proclaim for us as we desired, 'Bounteous is the Mindful Lord'. (51. 16)

It is not clear what was the nature and basis of Vishtaaspa's power in the land; perhaps it was simply wealth, perhaps it was the religious authority he possessed as a Kavi. The later Avesta tells of battles that he fought and defeats that he inflicted on various rivals.[47] If these stories have any historical basis, the inference would be that he had a fighting force at his disposal and used it to extend his control over a widening area.

This would have given Zoroaster's religion a foothold in the region. It may have spread further through missionary activity. The language of the *Gāthās*, in its transmitted form, perhaps contains clues to the route by which the faith spread to western Iran. It is coloured by traces of dialects of both the south-east (Arachosia, Drangiana) and the south-west (Persis or Persia proper). (See the map overleaf.) That suggests that the poems, and the religion founded upon them, were carried from their area of origin by the southern route via Kerman to the heart of Persis.

---

[47] *Yasht* 5. 105, 109–18; 9. 29–32; 19. 87.

Ancient Iran

This happened, we may presume, before the time of Darius' grandfather Arsames, if the surmise that he was a Zoroastrian is correct. From Persis the religion presently spread northwards into Media, to become the business of the priestly caste known as the Magi.

Meanwhile in the eastern territories, which by now must have been well seeded with Zoroastrian communities, priests were adding to the body of hymnic and liturgical compositions, producing the *Yashts* and other material that would eventually find a place in the Avesta. Their outlook on the world remained a provincial one. They took no notice of the momentous political developments taking place in the west, and so far as the surviving Avesta is concerned the Persian empire might never have existed. But while they continued to recite the *Gāthās* and the *Seven Chapters*, their religion was no longer quite what Zoroaster had taught. No new religion has the power to sweep away everything that has gone before, or so thoroughly to brainwash those who accept it that all their previous pieties are swept away. Compromises emerge between the new and the old. Already in the *Seven Chapters* we have seen some accommodation to popular religious sentiment, with worship extended not just to the abstract principles celebrated in the prophet's poems but also to the numinous elements of the physical world, the Earth, the Waters, the souls of all good people and of all harmless animals. In later Zoroastrianism such objects of veneration were formally recognized, not as Ahuras or Daēvas, but as *yazatas*, 'worshipful ones'.

The traditional gods were supposed to have been done away with, but in the Younger Avesta reverence is shown towards such figures as Mithra, the Sun and Moon, the wind god Vayu, the river goddess Ardvī Anāhitā, and others.[48] This is all in accord with Herodotus' statement (1. 131) that the Persians sacrifice to 'Zeus' (this must stand for Ahura Mazdā), whom they identify with the bright sky, and to Sun, Moon, Earth, Fire, Water, and Winds. By the later fifth century even royalty openly sanctioned such worship. Darius II (423–404) recognized the cult of Anāhitā, and his son Artaxerxes II (404–358) promoted her worship throughout the empire; in his inscriptions he includes

---

[48] See e. g. *Yashts* 5–10, 15; *Yasna* 25. 4–5.

the prayer 'May Auramazdā, Anāhitā, and Mithra protect me from all evil'.

Meanwhile an important modification had been made to Zoroaster's theology to deal with an anomaly that we noted earlier. The prophet had presented Spənta Manyu and Angra Manyu, the Bounteous and the Hostile Will, as a pair of twins, while in another poem Ahura Mazdā was called the father of the Bounteous Will. Was he then also the father of the Hostile Will? This was an unwelcome implication, since he was wholly good. A revised genealogy was accordingly produced in which Angra Manyu became the twin brother of Ahura Mazdā himself, both of them being represented as sons of the impartial deity Time (Zruvān). The dualism inherent in Zoroaster's thought was thus made absolute: a good and an evil power had existed side by side from the beginning, in constant conflict. This remained the fundamental doctrine of most later Zoroastrianism, in which the names of Ahura Mazdā and Angra Manyu lived on as Ohrmazd and Ahriman. The revised theology was bound up with the 12,000-year chronological scheme described earlier.

It was not only Zoroaster's theology that underwent modification and development after his death. Types of ritual flourished that he had openly condemned: the sacrifice of cattle, and the preparation and consumption of *haoma*. Evidently it was the sheer ethical force of his religion that powered its diffusion, the gospel of the Mindful Lord, Right, and Good Thought, and not the appeal of its austere forms of worship. Older practices continued and were integrated into Zoroastrian orthodoxy.

As the dominant religion of the Persian empire, upheld by the Achaemenid kings, Mazdaism flourished for two centuries, until the conquest by Alexander in 330 BCE. That brought the empire under Greek rule for some eighty years, and then it came under a Parthian dynasty, that of the Arsacids, which lasted till

226 CE. Little is known in detail about the fortunes of Zoroastrianism during these centuries. It survived, with much of its ancient literature, but it probably did not develop much, as the organization of the empire was less centralized than under the Achaemenids and local traditions of worship were rather left to look after themselves. There is evidence of increased official interest in the first or second century CE, when one or other of the various kings named Vologeses is said to have sent out instructions to each province to preserve its Zoroastrian texts and teachings as it had received them.

When the Arsacids gave way to the Sasanians, a royal line from Persia, the state took a firmer grip on religion. The first king, Ardashir I, is reported to have ordered that all written or oral records of Zoroastrian teaching be gathered together from all over Iran. His high priest Tansar then reviewed them and decided which ones were to be regarded as creditworthy. This was at least a step towards the establishment of a canonical Avesta.

For four centuries Zoroastrianism enjoyed its high summer of state-backed prestige, until in the mid seventh century Mesopotamia and Iran fell to the invading Muslim Arabs. This event did not destroy the native religion at once, but it dealt it a critical blow from which it never recovered. The cards were now stacked against it. Its adherents were suffered to exist but discriminated against in various ways, and increasing numbers of them converted to Islam.

Priestly study of the Avesta and religious writing in Pahlavi still continued for many generations. Much of our knowledge of Zoroastrian theology and legend is derived from Pahlavi works written in the ninth century or thereabouts. But there was little original writing after that. Further invasions of Iran by the Seljuk Turks and the Mongols between the eleventh and thirteenth centuries caused more extensive losses, including probably the disappearance of the greater part of the Avesta.

By this time a group of Zoroastrian émigrés had established themselves in Gujarat, which remained from then on the safest redoubt of the faith.

The transmission of the Gāthās

When we study the Greek or Latin classics we are dealing with works that have come down to us through a continuous written tradition. In most cases the manuscripts we have are no earlier than the Middle Ages, but they are copies of copies that go back ultimately to an original text written down or dictated by the ancient author. With the *Gāthās* the situation is similar in one regard, in that we are dependent on manuscripts, the oldest of which were written in the fourteenth century, but in other respects the case is very different. The written tradition in which these manuscripts stand began only in the Sasanian period. It is quite uncertain whether the *Gāthās* had ever been written down before then. The primary medium by which they were preserved for more than a thousand years from Zoroaster's time was oral transmission.

This is an astonishing fact, but a fact it almost certainly is. What is especially astonishing is the extraordinary fidelity with which, to all appearances, the original text was transmitted. It underwent gradual changes of pronunciation over the centuries, resulting in some superficial disruption of the metres. But the archaic vocabulary and grammar, only half understood by those who recited and heard the poems, were preserved intact. Such corruptions of the text as we can identify seem in nearly all cases to have arisen only during the period of written transmission.

The explanation of this state of affairs is that in Iran, as in India, it became the rule at an early date that priests committed large quantities of their sacred texts to memory, using various mnemonic techniques to ensure the strictest verbal accuracy, and recited or chanted them on the appropriate ritual occasions. In India the Vedas have been preserved in this way for the greater part of three thousand years. What proves the accuracy of their transmission is that a whole system of grammar and a whole system of accentuation, already obsolete in the classical Sanskrit of 500 BCE but authenticated by modern comparative philology, have survived in perfect shape. As with the *Gāthās*, changes of pronunciation over time have caused slight disturbance to the metres, but otherwise the text appears to be in virtually pristine condition.

In the light of our observations on the nature and occasion of Zoroaster's poems, it does not seem likely that he himself intended them to be memorized and perpetuated. It will have been his early disciples who decided that they should be regularly recited in association with the *Seven Chapters*, partly before, partly after. In this way the core of the traditional liturgy was established, and it became incumbent upon the officiating priests to know the texts by heart.

There was no possibility of writing them down because the country they lived in was illiterate. Until the Parthian period there existed, with one exception, no means of writing down any Iranian language. The exception was the customized cuneiform syllabary which the Achaemenid kings from the time of Darius I used for their royal inscriptions; but this had no wider currency. Late Zoroastrian writers have stories of how the Avesta was originally written down at the behest of Vishtaaspa, or how one of the later Dariuses had it inscribed on oxhides with gold ink in two copies, and how these ancient volumes were destroyed by Alexander. But these are certainly Sasanian myths, invented at a time when a tradition of written scriptures seemed a necessity for any respectable ancient religion.

Under the Arsacids the Aramaic alphabet was adapted for the writing of Parthian and other Middle Iranian languages. It is possible that some Avestan texts could have been written down in such a script. But it would have been an inadequate medium, and the written copies would have been of service only as an *aide-mémoire* for priests who had learned the texts orally. There is no reason to think that an entire written Avesta was produced at this period, or indeed that there was yet a recognized canon of texts constituting an Avesta. It was the Sasanian kings, so far as we know, who set in motion the project of drawing up such a canon and recording the constituent works in writing. This began, as mentioned above, under Ardashir in the third century. But the task of reducing the mass of material to order and producing an authoritative text extended over many generations. The oral tradition still retained the highest prestige. It was only in the reign of Khosrow I (531–578) that the high priest Veh-Shabuhr produced a definitive edition of the Avesta in 21 volumes and secured royal approval for it.

To record it in writing a special alphabet had been devised, and this is what is used in our manuscripts. It was based on the Pahlavi alphabet, but the number of characters was more than doubled, to a total of 53, in order to reflect meticulously every distinct phonetic nuance that was audible in the oral recitations by the priests. These nuances could not have been expressed in any earlier script, which proves that the Avesta text produced at this time was not dependent on a previous written tradition but newly based on the current oral tradition. The priests' pronunciation, however, had gradually changed over the centuries, without their being aware of it, to a point where it would have sounded very strange to Zoroaster. This Sasanian pronunciation is what our written text reflects. It is as if the *Canterbury Tales* had been been transmitted by purely oral means down to the twentieth century, the Middle English grammar and vocabulary being faithfully preserved but the pronunciation having evolved into something like a modern London accent, and the text so recited had then been recorded in the International Phonetic Alphabet. Western scholars have developed their own system for transliterating the Avestan script into an extended Latin alphabet. The extra symbols needed give it a singularly outlandish appearance. Here is how the first stanza of *Yasna* 28 appears in Avestan script (which runs from right to left) and in a modern edition:

ahiiā yāsā nəmaŋhā ustānazastō rafəδrahiiā
mainiiəuš mazdā pouruuīm spəṇtahiiā aṣā vīspə̄ṇg šiiaoϑnā
vaŋhə̄uš xratūm manaŋhō yā xšnəuuīšā gə̄ušcā uruuānəm.

The surviving manuscripts of the *Yasna* come partly from Iran and partly from India. They offer a virtually uniform text, the divergences among them being practically confined to trivial matters of orthography or casual error. However, the lack of serious variation does not mean that this text is reliable, because the archetype from which the manuscripts derive was a copy made several hundred years later than the Sasanian prototype. In the course of that time a certain number of mistakes had inevitably crept in.

The faulty nature of the transmission is evident from two omissions in the text of the *Gāthās*. In one poem a line is missing from one of the five-line stanzas (46. 15). In another, two stanzas have become conflated, with the loss of three and a half lines (53. 6). In other places we can infer from the metre that a word has been interpolated with the intention of clarifying the meaning. Sometimes the sense itself indicates or leads us to suspect that an error has occurred. In several passages it looks as if a word or a grammatical ending has been accidentally repeated from nearby, obliterating the true text. There is thus some scope for textual criticism and conjectural emendation. For those with a knowledge of Avestan I have provided at the end of the volume a list of variant or emended readings adopted for the purposes of the present translation.

Translating the Gāthās

The first challenge that faces any translator is that of understanding the meaning of the original. The *Gāthās* are notoriously difficult and problematic, and anyone who reckoned he had a sure understanding of every passage would be deluding himself. One has only to compare different modern versions with one another to see what a wide scope for disagreement there is among interpreters.

The difficulties are mainly lexical and syntactical. There are some words of whose meaning we have only an imprecise grasp, or no idea at all. There are many grammatical ambiguities, for example, whether a neuter noun ending in $-\bar{a}$ is a singular in the instrumental case or a plural in the nominative or accusative, and whether a verb form is a past tense or timeless in its reference (the so-called injunctive). There are even places where it is disputed whether a word is a noun or a verb. Often enough it is doubtful which word is to be construed with which, or where the boundaries of phrases and sentences lie.

It is not that Zoroaster intended to be riddling. His original hearers, we may suppose, being familiar with his language and with the poetic traditions that he drew on, already initiated in his doctrines, and hearing the poems intelligently delivered, will have had few serious problems of comprehension. I disagree fundamentally with those modern scholars who claim that the prophet's style is deliberately esoteric and encrypted, full of intentional double or multiple meanings. In my view, where different interpretations of a sentence are possible, it is the job of the translator or commentator to try to determine which one corresponds to the author's intention. To credit him with deliberate ambiguity or multivalence is merely an excuse for indecisiveness, or for showing off the commentator's resourcefulness.

In choosing between possible interpretations the best guide is contextual coherence. The translator must try to identify the essential thought underlying each sentence – what it is that Zoroaster is wanting to say and striving to express in metrical form – and to trace the sequence of his thinking from stanza to stanza. The more coherent the sequence of thought that can be elicited, while interpreting the words in as unforced a way as possible, the more likely it will be that we have reached a correct understanding.

In interpreting individual sentences the translator must try to cultivate a sense for natural word groupings and typical structural patterns, and a sense of the relationship between phrase and verse. He must also respect the order in which words and phrases are presented, which was, after all, the order in which Zoroaster's hearers received them and mentally processed them. In my version I have so far as possible made each line of the English correspond to a line of the original, believing that this is the best way of conveying the structure of the prophet's utterances. Here and there, for clarity, I have supplied in the English, in brackets, a word that is left implicit in the original.

The coherence that the translator believes he discerns will not always be immediately obvious to the reader. In order to make it clearer I have followed the example of Jacques Duchesne-Guillemin[49] and provided for each poem, facing the translation, a stanza-by-stanza paraphrase. This will at least show how I interpret the text in its main outlines.

In translating words that recur in different passages, especially those denoting specifically Zoroastrian concepts, a balance has to be struck between the ideal of consistency and the requirements of the individual context. With terms such as Aša and Ārmati it is practicable to stick to 'Right' and 'Piety' throughout. But there are others which it is not feasible always to render by the same English word. For *xšaϑra*-, for instance, I have mostly used 'dominion', but there are places where 'domain', 'realm', 'command', 'rule', 'reign', 'sway', 'power', 'control', 'domination', or 'authority' seemed more appropriate. I have tried to avoid haphazardness on the one hand and mechanical equivalences on the other.

Finally it must be emphasized that any translation of the *Gāthās* necessarily has a provisional character. The translator does his best, but in the end he remains acutely aware of all the obscurities he has failed to clarify and all the alternative possibilities he has not definitively eliminated. I have often been struck by the truth of H. S. Nyberg's dictum: 'whoever has dealt with these texts has resigned himself to translate differently in the morning from what he did the night before'. Here and there, where a rendering is particularly open to question, I have indicated as much by setting the doubtful word or phrase in italics. But without writing a detailed commentary it is impossible to signal all the uncertainties to the reader, who is accordingly warned not to take everything too much on trust.

---

[49] *The Hymns of Zarathustra* (London 1952).

The Hymns of Zoroaster
(The *Gāthās*)

YASNA 28

The poem follows the form of a traditional supplication to gods, reverently uttered with hands upraised, to come into the worshipper's presence and give assistance.

(1) Zoroaster prays for supportive intervention from above. As its primary source he emphasizes the Positive Will, that is, the impulse that chooses good over evil (cf. *Yasna* 30 and 45 for the significance of the Positive Will). Within this opening stanza he mentions all three of his favourite divine entities, the Mindful One, Right, and Good Thought. He prays for an intervention that will make it possible to fulfil what Good Thought, in its wisdom, requires for the alleviation of the cow's distress; to understand what this refers to one must read the following poem, *Yasna* 29.

(2–4) Zoroaster affirms his devotion to the three entities, holding that their power in the world is increased by human piety (3), and that goodness (born of good thought) is rewarded and badness punished (4). But at present he is looking for material as well as spiritual benefit: a change of circumstances that will give him and his followers the status they want (2).

28.1

I pray You all in reverence with outstretched hands for his help —
the Bounteous Will's in first place, Mindful One, with Right —
    through action
by which Thou wouldst satisfy Good Thought's wisdom and the
    cow's soul:

2

I who will approach You, Mindful Lord, with good thought,
to give me of both existences, the material one and that of
    thought,
those blessings in line with Right by which one could keep one's
    supporters in well-being;

3

I who will hymn You, Right and Good Thought, as never before
and the Mindful Lord, You whose unimpaired dominion also
is increased by Piety: come to my calls to give help.

4

I who have taken my soul in mind for praise-song together with
    Good Thought,
and knowing the Mindful Lord's repayments for actions,
so long as I have the ability and strength, will look out in search
    of Right.

(5) In his quest for Right he will cultivate good thought and compliance, that is, the habit of listening to and following the guidance that good thought gives. This creates a place or a way in for the Mindful Lord, enabling him to be recognized as the supreme authority. By insisting on these principles Zoroaster has the best hope of persuading the oppressors to mend their ways.

(6–7) A string of direct requests to the divine powers, some general, others referring specifically to the situation in which Zoroaster wants help. To his own name he appends 'and us', meaning probably his whole group of supporters, the ones alluded to in stanza 2. But in the next stanza he names another individual, his influential patron Vishtaaspa, the man in whom his hopes chiefly rest. The Mindful One is asked to prove his concern by providing Zoroaster with an effective 'mantra' or prescript, perhaps meaning the one that was to overcome the enemy in stanza 5.

(8) A somewhat empty stanza, added for the sake of bringing in the name of Frashaushtra, an associate of Vishtaaspa who appears in several other poems (*Yasna* 46, 49, 51, 53).

5

O Right, shall I see Thee, as I acquire good thought
and, as a path[1] for the most mighty Lord, the Mindful One,
  compliance?
Through this prescript may we convince the predators[2] most
  fully with our tongue.

6

Come with Good Thought, give with Right Thy enduring gift
in upright utterances, Mindful One, strong support for Zara-
  thushtra
and for us (all), Lord, with which we may overcome the foe's
  acts of enmity.

7

Give, O Right, that reward, the blessings of good thought;
give Thou, Piety, enablement to Vishtaaspa and myself;
give Thou, Mindful One, showing Thy authority, the prescript
  in which we might hear Your caring.

8

For the best gift, Best One who art of one mind with best Right,
Lord, I pray Thee earnestly on behalf of the upstanding Frashaush-
  tra and myself
and those on whom Thou mayest bestow it for ever out of Good
  Thought.

---

[1] Or: place, seat.
[2] The word properly denotes animal marauders such as wolves. Here (as in 34. 5 and 9)
  it stands for the wrongful men who harass the cow.

(9) Zoroaster begins to round off his poem. He expresses the hope that his importunities will not irritate the addressees. A parallel in the Rigveda (2. 33. 4) suggests that this was a traditional motif in Indo-Iranian prayers that Zoroaster is using for the sake of form. Again he names his trinity, the Mindful Lord, Right, and Good Thought, ascribing to them the power of strengthening their devotees.

(10) He emphasizes the worthiness of the supplicants, and asks for them to be given what they want. This is again a conventional element in prayer hymns.

(11) Zoroaster concludes with a reference to his own role as the Mindful Lord's hymnist. He hopes that the Lord will inspire him to compose poems embodying teachings that will do justice to the highest truths and will promote the restoration of the original, perfect state of existence.

9

With these prayers may we not anger You, Lord, nor Right
and Best Thought, we who are busy offering Your praises:
Ye are the promptest ones; Your powers and domain are of
   strengths.

10

Those then whom Thou knowest to be upright before Right and
   Good Thought
and worthy, Mindful Lord, fulfil their desire with attainment;
I know that well-purposed hymns of devotion to You are not in
   vain.

11

Thou who with their aid dost protect Thy Right and Good
   Thought for ever,
teach me, Mindful Lord, to voice in line with Thy will
through Thy mouth (those teachings) by which the pristine ex-
   istence may come about.

YASNA 29

This remarkable composition is concerned with the tribulations of cattle-owners in Zoroaster's society. He adverts to the topic in several other poems (31. 9–10, 32. 8–14, 33. 4, 44. 6, 20, 51. 14), where it appears that cattle are repeatedly driven off from their pastures and condemned to sacrifice. Here he imagines the feelings of the cow herself and frames them into an appeal to the powers above, which leads to a concerned debate among them.

(1) As a cow does not have the faculty of speech, Zoroaster does not put words in her mouth but in her mind; it is her soul that articulates them. They are nevertheless heard by the addressees. She finds herself in circumstances at odds with her presumed role in life and with the purposeful design that she assumes in the world. Who then created her, and for whose benefit? As those around her cannot guarantee good pasturing for her, let those above see to it.

(2) Her cause is taken up by her maker in heaven. What, he asks Right, is the answer to the mismatch she complains of? She and her herdsman are meant to conduct a peaceful pastoral life, and yet they are continually beset by Wrong's violent followers. Who is to protect her and drive them away?

(3) Right, while in no way out of accord with the others, and not unsympathetic to the cow, replies in non-committal terms. He does not see clearly what the answer is. It is the role of the upright to assist the weak and stimulate them to resistance, but they do that at the instance of another, higher being who exercises the supreme power, and whom Right will attend when he makes his requirements known: (4) this is the Mindful Lord, who possesses an all-embracing knowledge of past and future circumstances. He will consider the matter, as he considers everything, in the light of that; but it will be his decision, and it will have to be accepted, however it goes.

29.1

To You the cow's soul complains: 'For whom did Ye shape me?
Who made me?
Fury and force, cruelty, violence, and aggression hold me bound.
I have no pastor but You; so show Yourselves in good pasturing.'

2

Then the Maker of the Cow asks Right: 'How was Thy ruling for
the cow,
when Ye powers put her there? Cattle-tending lies with the
pastor;
(but) whom did Ye want to be her lord, that might repulse fury
by the wrongful?'

3

To him Right, no breacher of unity, no enemy of the cow, will
answer:
'Of those things there is no knowing. He by whom the upright
invigorate the weak
is the mightiest of beings; to his calls I will respond, *my ear reaches
no further*:

4

'the Mindful One, the most heedful of initiatives, both those
taken in the past
by Daevas and mortals, and those that may be taken hereafter.
He is the lord that judges; it will be as He will.'

(5) This response has not resolved the problem. Zoroaster now joins the cow and questions the Mindful Lord directly in his own person.

(6) The Mindful Lord replies, addressing the cow. His answer covers her original questions as to who made her and for whom, and her maker's questions as to whether there is any protector appointed for her. There is none, because her maker (now called Thworshtar, the Shaper, a traditional figure corresponding to the Vedic creator Tvashtr) put her in the charge of the cattle-breeder and herdsman and left it to them to uphold her interests.

(7) Here Zoroaster reverts to his own voice. There, he says, you have the Mindful Lord's righteous ordinance. The cow is there to provide dairy products (not meat, as the sacrificers think). In his bounty he has provided for dairy farming to feed the hungry. But at present its benefits, as conceived in heaven, are withheld from the earth. If the cow has no divine patron, whom can the Lord suggest as the agent who, guided by good thought, will be able to put things right?

5

But we two are here with outstretched hands propitiating the
   Lord,
my soul and the milch cow's, as we put the Mindful One to our
   questions:
'Is there no prospect for the righteous-living one, none for the
   stock-raiser, among the wrongful?'

6

Then the Lord speaks, the Mindful One, knowing the designs in
   his wisdom:
'Indeed no patron has (yet) been found, nor a ruling in line with
   Right;
the Shaper has created thee for the stock-raiser and the herds-
   man.'

7

Milk and butter, this is the prescript that the Lord, of one mind
   with Right, made
for the cow, He the Mindful One; He is bounteous to the needy
   through his teaching.
— Whom hast Thou who by good thought could establish those
   things for mortals?

(8) The Mindful Lord replies, not speaking specifically to Zoroaster but making a pronouncement before the whole company involved in the dialogue; it is heard equally by the cow. He says that there is just one such person, namely Zoroaster, who listens to the higher powers' guidance and composes poems promoting their cause. His poetry is like a well-built chariot that the Mindful Lord harnesses to his racing steeds for victory.[3]

(9) But this exchange has still not solved the original problem, and the cow resumes her lament. It is not sufficient to have Zoroaster as her champion, as he lacks influence. When will there be someone with the means to back up his teaching with a show of force? (10) She prays for Zoroaster and his supporters to be given the strength and authority necessary for the maintenance of peaceful conditions. She has trust in the Mindful Lord and looks to him to provide.

(11) Zoroaster concludes in his own voice. As things are, that combination of authority with right and good thought is not in evidence. Why are they not to be seen here? Zoroaster declares that he himself is the one who may be able to bring about reform, the one whom the Mindful Lord must prepare and sponsor for a certain critical event that is to come. Let his and his followers' devotion now be repaid with support from above.

---

[3] That this is the metaphor is suggested by 30. 10 and 50. 7. Similar imagery occurs in the Rigveda and in Greek poets.

8

'This man here I have found, the only one who listens to Our
teachings:
Zarathushtra Spitāma. He desires, mindful, on Our behalf and
Right's,
to broadcast Our praises, as I harness his well-constructed utter-
ance.'

9

Yet the cow's soul laments, 'That I am to put up with an ineffec-
tive carer,
the voice of a powerless man, whom I wish enabled with author-
ity!
When will there ever be one who will give him physical assis-
tance?

10

'Grant Ye them, Lord, strength with right, and that authority
with Good Thought, by which one may establish fair dwelling
and peace:
I for one realize Thee, Mindful One, to be the first procurer of
that.'

11

Where are Right and Good Thought and Dominion? It is me,
with Right,
that Ye in Your providence must acknowledge, Mindful One,
for the great rite.
Lord, (come) down to us now, in return for our liberality, Your
followers'.

YASNA 30

This is a poetical sermon addressed to those who have gathered to hear it (the 'proselytes' of the first line; cf. 45. 1, 47. 6), or more broadly to mankind at large (final stanza).

(1) Zoroaster is proclaiming a message of importance to everybody, whether they have heard it before or not. It is headed by the naming of the familiar trinity, the Mindful Lord, Good Thought, and Right. They are to be celebrated with praise, thoughtful worship, and cheerful activity in the light of day (cf. 32. 10).

(2) The audience must not just hear the prophet's words but ponder his message. The choice is between good and evil. Everyone has to make this choice for himself, but he should be aware that he will one day have to account for himself to the Mindful Lord, and that reward and punishment will be dispensed.

(3) Good and evil now assume more definite form as a pair of opposed Wills or Mentalities (*manyū*). They came into being in the beginning, they make their way into people's minds as voices in dreams, and they manifest themselves in the contrasting tendencies of human thought, speech, and action. Much depends on making the right choice between them.

(4) From the first occasion when they contest with each other in a man's mind, he is faced with decisions that will determine his ultimate fate; he becomes either a Wrong-follower (*drəgvant-*) or a Right-follower (*ašavan-*).

30.1

Now I will speak, O proselytes, of what ye may bring to the
    attention even of one who knows,
praises for the Lord and Good Thought's acts of worship
well considered, and for Right; the gladness beheld by the day-
    light.

2

Hear with your ears the best message, behold with lucid mind
the two choices in the decision each man makes for his own
    person
before the great Supplication, as ye look ahead to the declaration
    to Him.

3

They are the two Wills, the twins who in the beginning made
    themselves heard through dreaming,
those two kinds of thought, of speech, of deed, the better and
    the evil;
and between them well-doers discriminate rightly, but ill-doers
    do not.

4

Once those two Wills join battle, a man adopts
life or non-life, the way of existence that will be his at the last:
that of the wrongful the worst kind, but for the righteous one,
    best thought.

(5) The two Wills are now labelled the Wrongful one and the Bounteous or Positive one. The latter is picturesquely described as clothing himself in adamant, literally 'the hardest stones'; that is, he is Right's warrior who wears impenetrable armour and cannot be killed. He always opts for the true and good, as do all who act rightly and so please the Mindful Lord.

(6) The Daevas, the traditional gods of Iran whom Zoroaster has replaced with his own moral-intellectual deities, but who still guide (and here stand for) the aggressive groups that harass his community, make the wrong choice from lack of clear thinking, and swarm to commit acts of violence. People who do this afflict the life of the world as with a disease.

(7) The alternative is to build up the Mindful Lord's power by allying oneself with Good Thought and Right. This results in health and vigour of body and soul, and the outcome will be that the Mindful Lord will hold the chieftain of the evil ones, namely the Wrongful Will, fettered and impotent. (8) When that time comes and they are made to pay for their crimes, the Mindful One (and his representatives on earth) will be left exercising their right-thinking sovereignty and proclaiming it to all who battle against and defeat the forces of Wrong.

5

Of those two Wills, the Wrongful one chooses to do the worst
things,

but the most Bounteous Will (chooses) Right, he who clothes
himself in adamant;

as do those also who committedly please the Lord with genuine
actions, the Mindful One.

6

Between those two the very Daevas fail to discriminate rightly,
because delusion

comes over them as they deliberate, when they choose worst
thought;

they scurry together to the violence with which mortals blight
the world.

7

But suppose one comes with dominion for Him, with good
thought and right,

then vitality informs the body, piety the soul:

their ringleader Thou wilt have as if in irons:

8

and when the requital comes for their misdeeds,

for Thee, Mindful One, together with Good Thought, will be
found dominion

to proclaim to those, Lord, who deliver Wrong into the hands
of Right.

(9) May we be the ones who accomplish this and see the world restored to its ideal condition! – Such is the prayer that Zoroaster addresses to the Mindful Lord and Right and his other deities, to whom he here applies a specially coined epithet meaning probably 'bringers of change'. In striving to achieve the victory we must focus our minds in those areas where we do not yet see clearly and continuously, where the two Wills are still tussling.

(10) When the victory comes, those who have prospered under Wrong will be ruined. The contest for fame and glory, pictured metaphorically as a horse race, will be won by those from the stables of the Mindful One, Good Thought, and Right.

(11) So, people, you must learn, by experience and by observation of your own and others' successes and failures, the principle that governs life: Right prospers in the end, and Wrong suffers. If you take that to heart and act on it, the future that we hope for can be brought about.

9

May we be the ones who will make this world splendid,
Mindful One and Ye Lords, bringers of change, and Right,
as our minds come together where insight is fluctuating.

10

For then destruction will come down upon Wrong's prosperity,
and the swiftest (steeds) will be yoked from the fair dwelling of
  Good Thought,
of the Mindful One, and of Right, and they will be the winners
  in good repute.

11

When ye grasp those rules that the Mindful One lays down,
  O mortals,
through success and failure, and the lasting harm that is for the
  wrongful
as furtherance is for the righteous, then thereafter desire will be
  fulfilled.

YASNA 31

This longer sermon is for the most part formally addressed to the Mindful One, though the human audience is acknowledged towards the end. The opening (1) seems to pick up from the close of *Yasna* 30 with its mention of the Mindful Lord's rules. They are the basis of Zoroaster's message, which the wrongdoers ignore but which offers the greatest rewards to the faithful.

(2) If Zoroaster's words are not sufficient to make it clear which is the right path, he appeals to the powers above to confirm the contrasted fates that the Lord has established for the righteous and the wrongful, to persuade people to live in accord with truth.

(3) The Mindful One himself is invited to state the nature of these contrasted fates, which are allocated with the help of fire; by reporting his words Zoroaster hopes to convert everyone. (But the clear statement is held back to the end of the poem, stanza 20.)

(4) This stanza develops the theme of the prophet's ministry. When the time comes, he will call upon all the higher powers, including the figure of Reward that is central to his present message, and petition them to extend his influence in the land and overcome Wrong.

31.1

Minding these rules of Yours, we proclaim words unheeded
by those who with the rules of Wrong are disrupting Right's
flock,
but the best for those who will trust in the Mindful One.

2

If hereby the better way is not in plain view to the soul,
then I appeal to You all according to the ruling known to the
Lord, the Mindful One,
(the ruling) on those two lots, so that we may live in accord with
Right.

3

The atonement that Thou didst establish with Thy will and with
fire and with Right assign to the two parties,
the rule that is for the prudent – tell us that, Mindful One, for
our knowledge
with the tongue of Thy mouth, and with it may I convince
everyone alive.

4

When the time comes to invoke Right and the Mindful One and
the Lords
with Reward and Piety, I shall petition with best thought
for a strong authority for myself, by whose increase we might
vanquish Wrong.

(5) After this slight digression the Mindful One is asked again to declare what the better fate is that the faithful can expect (and by implication the alternative that will face their antagonists).

(6) A reply comes, though not a very explicit one. It will go best for the one who knows and proclaims the reality that the Mindful Lord represents: this is the recipe for an existence not diminished by sickness, corrupted by wrong, or cut short by premature death. Such a preacher, as he widens his influence (as Zoroaster hopes to, stanza 4), builds up the Mindful One's dominion.

(7) Those blessings are to be enjoyed in the light of day, in this life under the sun, where The Mindful One created them in the beginning by his intellect. He also created Right, which sustains Good Thought; here is Zoroaster's regular trinity, with their relationships defined. The Mindful One's beneficent and purposeful will remains unchanged to this day, and by exercising it he grows ever greater.

(8) Zoroaster continues his reflections on the Mindful One's first creation, imagining him as a young deity, fathering Good Thought and fashioning Right, and all the while presiding over the world's doings.

5

Tell me, so I may distinguish it, that better lot Ye appointed for
    me with Right,
so I may know and take to heart with Good Thought, whose
    prophet (I am),
those things, Mindful Lord, that will not be, or will be.

6

– 'It will go best for him who knows and speaks my truth,
the prescript of health, right, and continuing life.
What he increases for Him through good thought, that is domin-
    ion for the Mindful One.'

7

He who first conceived these amenities permeating the world of
    light,
He by his sapience is the creator of Right, with which He upholds
    Best Thought.
Through that will, Mindful One, Thou dost increase, which even
    unto now, Lord, is the same.[4]

8

I think of Thee first, Mindful One, as being young in my thought,
the father of Good Thought, when I catch Thee in my eye,
the true creator of Right,[5] lord over the world's doings.

4 Or 'who . . . art the same.'
5 Or, with an emended reading, 'the companion of Right (and) creator'.

(9) Within this cosmogonic frame Zoroaster brings in another of his favourite topics, the cow and her place in the world. The Mindful One, here identified as her maker, showed his wisdom and right thinking by letting her choose whether to be in the herdsman's care or that of others. (10) She chose the righteous herdsman as her master, and showed no favour to the non-herdsman who tries to disturb the proper ordering of things by driving her away for his own ungodly purposes.

(11) Zoroaster now begins working back to his main theme, easing the transition by remaining for the moment in creationist mode. The Mindful One equipped us with bodies and minds, moral outlooks, the faculties of speech and action, and the power of choice.

(12) When a choice is to be made, a man hears inner voices urging him to go one way or the other (the two conflicting Wills described in *Yasna* 30); the knowing one speaks aright, the uninstructed one speaks falsely. Considered another way, it is a dialogue between Piety and the undecided man's personal will.

9

Thine was piety, Thine too was the cow-fashioner sapience
of will, Mindful Lord, when Thou gavest her a path
to come either on the herdsman's side or (on his) who is not a
herdsman.

10

But she of these two chose the herdsman, the stock-raiser
as her lord, the righteous one, the cultivator of good thought:
the non-herdsman, Mindful One, drive her as he might, did not
get her goodwill.

11

Since first, Mindful One, Thou didst fashion our living bodies
and moral selves
with Thy thought, and our intellects, since Thou gavest bodily
vitality
and actions and pronouncements, (it has been the case that)
where the free agent makes his choices,

12

there it may be one of false words who speaks forth, or one of
straight words,
one with knowledge or one without it, through that man's heart
and thought:
point for point Piety debates with the will where there is hesita-
tion.

(13) But whether it is a matter involving such an inner struggle, or an open debate, or – here Zoroaster throws in an apparently unrelated topic, but one that must be on his mind in his actual situation – a case of excessive punishment by the authorities for a small transgression, all these things are taken note of by the Mindful One.

(14) Zoroaster reprises his questions about things to come. When the time of reckoning comes, how will the righteous one and the wrongful be repaid for their respective contributions? (15) What is the punishment for those who foster the power of the malevolent cattle-raiders?

(16) We expect, 'and what is the reward for the good who defend them?' But Zoroaster is diverted into a more pressing question about the good contender in the power struggle, the wealthy and pious man who will use his means to acquire retainers and build up his own area of control. When will such a man appear on the scene? What will he see fit to do?

13

The questioning that is overt, Mindful One, or the secrets that
    the two (voices) debate,
or if someone for a minor misdeed receives the greatest punish-
    ment –
all those things, watchful with Thy flashing eye, Thou regardest
    with Right.

14

I ask Thee, Lord, about the things that are approaching and will
    come,
the requitals that will be given of gifts from the righteous one
and those from the wrongful, Mindful One – how they will be
    at the Reckoning.

15

I ask this: what the punishment is for him who is initiating
    dominion for the wrongful one,
for the evil-doer, Lord, who cannot find a livelihood without
wronging the herdsman that is innocent before man and beast.

16

I ask this: how that munificent man who is zealous to promote
    with Right
his authority over house or district or region,
one of Thine, Mindful Lord – when he will be there, and how
    acting.

(17) Meanwhile the promoters of the right and wrong doctrines compete. Let the enlightened instruct the enlightened, that is, let the (partly) enlightened take their instruction from the enlightened, and listen no longer to the misleading talk of the unenlightened. Let the Mindful One guide our thinking in the right paths.

(18) Do not give a hearing to the spokesmen of Wrong (priests of the old religion, with their demands for animal sacrifices?), who will ruin our local economy and way of life. No, take up your axes and attack them!

(19) Listen instead to the enlightened and eloquent devotee of Right, who improves life rather than impairing it, in preparation for that time of reckoning when (as already signalled in stanza 3) the Mindful One, deploying his flaming fire, will allocate the blessings he has to bestow between the two parties, the righteous and the wrongful.

(20) Now at last we hear what their fates consist of. Those who come to hear and join the true prophet will enter a realm of light and bliss. The wrongful will find themselves in a place of lasting darkness and woe, with only foul food to eat.

17

Which is to be the more persuasive, the righteous one or the
  wrongful?
Let the knowing one speak to the knowing; let the unknowing
  delude no longer.
Be for us, Mindful Lord, our teacher of good thought.

18

Let none of you listen to the wrongful one's prescripts and
  teachings,
for he will give house or manor or district or region
into chaos and ruin; so cut them down with the axe.

19

Let him listen (rather) to him who has thought on Right, a healer
  of existence, a knowing one, Lord,
who for true voicing of words is free master of his tongue
under Thy flaming fire, Mindful One, when the good is allocated
  between the two parties.

20

Whoso comes to the righteous one, radiance is his to possess
  hereafter;
(but) a long age of darkness, foul food, cries of woe by way of
  speech,
that is the existence to which, ye wrongful, through your own
  actions your morality will bring you.

(21) So that we may achieve that conjunction of life, health, and rightness which is the most desirable state under the sun (stanzas 6–7), the Mindful Lord bestows from his bounty, upon people of good will and good actions, the gift of consistent good thought, which is the essential quality that keeps us on the right road.

(22) Equipped with this good thought, the well-doer sees all these things clearly. In all that he says and does, he keeps firm hold on right. He will dwell with the Mindful Lord, and be most welcome in his abode.

21

The Mindful Lord gives, for the union of health and continuing
    life
and rightness, from His rich sovereign domain,
the permanence of good thought to him who is His ally in will
    and deeds.

22

These things are clear for the well-doer even as he apprehends
    them in his mind:
he with good command holds on to Right in word and deed.
He, O Mindful Lord, shall be Thy most welcome house-guest.

YASNA 32

The dominant theme of this poem is the opposition between the good people who inhabit Zoroaster's region and the wrongful Daeva-worshippers who disrupt their peaceful lives with their thefts of cattle.

(1) Zoroaster begins with the hypothetical vision of a whole tribal region united in devotion to the Mindful Lord; even its old gods, the Daevas, submit to him in Zoroaster's imagination. All declare their readiness to spread the Lord's gospel and confound his enemies.

(2) The Mindful Lord for his part, supported by his regular partners Good Thought and Right,[6] and enjoying the dominion that he draws from the piety of the faithful, acknowledges their virtuous character and declares that he and they are united in their outlook.

(3) But now Zoroaster contrasts the vision with the reality, addressing the unregenerate Daevas. They are the offspring of the opposites of Good Thought and Right, namely Evil Thought and Wrong, and of Contempt or Arrogance, qualities that character-ize the conduct of the man of power and influence who follows them. (Probably one particular such man is here in view.) From the same wellsprings come the evil deeds that have made them notorious over the whole land.[7]

(4) Some of the worst things that men do are done in order to satisfy the demands of the Daevas (for sacrifices) and to win their greater favour. But by such actions they are turning away from the Mindful Lord, Good Thought, and Right.

---

[6] Right is here called 'sunny' or 'sunlit' from its association with the light of day; cf. stanza 10, and 31. 7; 53. 4.

[7] 'Earth's seventh part' refers to a mythical geography found in the Younger Avesta (e.g. *Yasht* 10. 133), by which the earth is divided into seven *karšvars* or (arable) lands.

32.1

Suppose for His the clan prays, for His the village with the tribe,
for His the Daevas, in my fancy, for the Mindful Lord's gladden-
    ing, (saying)
'We will be Thy messengers, to demolish those who hate You':

2

to them the Mindful Lord, united with Good Thought,
answers as befits his authority, as the good friend of Right the
    sunlit,
'Your liberal piety, as it is good, We adopt: it shall be Ours!'

3

But ye Daevas are all spawned from Evil Thought,
as is the grandee who worships you, and from Wrong and Con-
    tempt;
your duplicitous deeds too, for which ye have become renowned
    in earth's seventh part,

4

ever since ye have been enjoining those worst of things that
    mortals are to do
to wax in the Daevas' favour, retreating from Good Thought,
losing the way from the Mindful Lord's wisdom and from Right.

(5) In prompting men to do these things, the Daevas are seducing them away from the peaceful settled existence in which they are (relatively) secure from premature death. The Daevas themselves are misled by the Evil Will, who makes them think evil; and hence comes the evil speech with which that Evil Will induces the wrongdoer to take over responsibility for the evil deed.

(6) From here on Zoroaster speaks no more of the Daevas, only of the human evildoer(s). The powerful man is guilty of many offences against peace in his efforts to win a name for himself (as a warrior, or as a patron of great sacrificial banquets). But these offences are known to the Mindful Lord, who keeps all men's deserts in mind. Wherever he and Right are respected, let his edict be broadcast, namely that the good will be rewarded hereafter and the bad punished.

(7) According to this edict the outrages aforementioned – of which Zoroaster declares his own innocence – are capital offences, which, following the trial of the sinner by molten metal, will be visited with the severe penalty that the Mindful Lord ordains.

(8) These evil practices of cow-slaughter go back to Yima, the mythical institutor of animal sacrifice. Zoroaster, being innocent of them, is content to submit himself to the Mindful Lord's judgment.

5

So ye lure the mortal from good living and security from death,
as the Evil Will does you who are Daevas, by evil thought
and that evil speech with which he assigns the deed to the wrongful
one's control.

6

The many offences against peace by which he seeks renown (if
that is what he is doing),
O Lord that rememberest our deserts, Thou knowest with Best
Thought.
In Thy domain, Mindful One, and Right's let Your decree be
given out.

7

Of such offences I declare I know nothing in my rectitude,
which are decreed mortal, for which one is tried by the glowing
metal,
and of whose consequences Thou, Mindful Lord, art the para-
mount provider.

8

For such offences Vivahvant's son was renowned, even Yima,
who sought to gratify our mortal race by feeding them portions
of the cow.
As to these deeds, I rest on Thy decision, Mindful One.

(9) Those who instigate such activities pervert the good fame that the warrior class aspires to, turning it into infamy; they pervert the intelligence proper to living creatures, and deny Zoroaster the fulfilment of purposes inspired by good thought.[8] Such are the thoughts that he is moved to express to the Mindful Lord as he protests at the actions of the wrongful.

(10) Yes, they pervert good fame, those who teach people to hate the sight of the cow living peacefully in the light of the sun and to take her away for slaughter; who induce good men to do evil things, disrupt pastoral life, and attack the innocent cattle-breeders and herdsmen.

(11) They, if anyone, are the perverters of life, those preachers of wrong and their patrons; for what is it but perversion, to seek to deprive respectable men and women of their rightful possessions, and to seduce people of honest nature away from right thinking?

(12) What they see as a heroic exploit adding to their fame and repute, when it leads other men to do bad things, in fact brings them ill repute with the Mindful Lord. Here is more perversion: of the cow's existence as they drive her away from her pastures, and of the Karpan priest's due devotion to Right as they induce him to accept the feasting on beef(?) and subjection to masters who promulgate Wrong.

---

[8] The interpretation of these lines is uncertain.

9

The false teacher perverts good repute, perverts life's reason
    with his pronouncements;
he robs me of the capability esteemed of Good Thought.
These plaints of my will, Mindful One, I utter to Right and to
    You (all).

10

That is the man who perverts good repute, who declares that the
    worst thing to behold
with the eyes is the cow, and the sun; and he who makes the
    upright wrongful,
and he who despoils the pastures, and he who raises his weapon
    against the righteous one.

11

They are the ones that pervert life, the wrongful who, with the
    grandees, have distinguished themselves
by depriving matrons and masters of the possession of their
    inheritance,
and who will divert the righteous, Mindful One, from best
    thought.

12

Because of the 'deed of repute' by which they divert mortals
    from best action,
the Mindful One answers them with ill, who pervert the cow's
    life by shouting 'Move along!'
and with whom the Karpan chooses *gluttony* instead of right, and
    the dominion of those who promote wrong,

(13) The result of this subjection will be that they will end up condemned to dwell for ever in the House of Evil Thought,[9] for corrupting this life of ours and opposing the message of Zoroaster, the Mindful Lord's 'mantra-man'. This they do from an appetite that will not allow them to see Right, (14) an appetite that holds them fast, so that they, and even the Kavi priests, constantly give in to it and surrender their reason to it, as they assist with the rites of cow-sacrifice, presided over by the impious master of ceremonies who pours into the fire the libation of the holy juice (*haoma*, = the Indian *soma*) pressed from a certain mountain plant.

(15) In cooperating with these activities the Karpans and Kavis have gone astray. The innocent people whom they force to play a part in them, such as the stock-raisers compelled to provide animals as victims, will not share their fate hereafter, but will go to live in the House of Good Thought.

---

[9] Elsewhere called the House of Wrong (46. 11; 49. 11; 51. 14).

13

the dominion by which the *glutton* bids to stand in the house of
Worst Thought:
the destroyers of this existence, and those, Mindful One, who
decry in their lust
Thy prophet's message, (the lust) that will keep them from the
sight of Right.

14

Into its bonds the *glutton*, the very Kavis surrender their reason
and their dignity daily, when they stand ready to assist the wrong-
ful one
and when the cow is spoken for killing, (the wrongful one) who
makes the resistant juice flare up.

15

By these activities the Karpanhood and the Kavihood have lost
their way.
Those whom they implicate in them, not being in free control of
their lives,[10]
will be borne away from them both into the house of Good
Thought.

---

[10] I.e. the innocent cattle-farmers forced to cooperate with the authorities who demand
cow sacrifices.

(16) The difficult final stanza, which contains thoughts and vocabulary not paralleled elsewhere in the *Gāthās*, brings a suitably optimistic conclusion to the poem, though one that does not connect clearly with what has gone before. Zoroaster seems to revert to the wishful thinking of the opening. He imagines a country made safe by a strong, enlightened ruler, where the bad people will run into trouble at every turn and their endeavours will come to grief.

16

There is nothing finer than if one just draws back to the *safe haven*
  of the enlightened one,
in control, Mindful Lord, of that whose danger is a threat.
Whatever is for the wrongful one's hurt, I will set in place[11]
  throughout the desirable people.

---

[11] The image may be of setting ambushes.

YASNA 33

This is one of Zoroaster's most personal and inward-looking poems. He addresses no one but the divine entities and makes no reference to current tensions or conflicts. His subject is his own piety and his claims to receive his due reward from the Mindful One. We have the impression that he is well on in years and looking towards the end of his life.

The first three stanzas are couched in general terms. (1) The principles laid down for the original existence continue to be applied: people will receive their just deserts according to whether their lives have been good, bad, or some mixture of the two. (2) It matters how one acts towards other good or bad people. One gains credit with the Mindful Lord for opposing the bad by any means, including physical encounter, or by showing others how to be good; (3) if one assists the righteous, not only those of one's own clan but across wider social networks, and looks after the cattle properly, one will be looked after oneself with equal care by Right and Good Thought.

(4) Zoroaster now focuses on his personal qualifications, stating some of them initially in a series of parallel relative clauses. By his worship he strives to counter a cluster of evils: failure to hearken to the Mindful Lord, bad thought, hybristic attitudes, opprobrium, anti-pastoral acts. To emphasize the country-wide scope of his concerns he repeats the list of arenas from the preceding stanza – clan, village community, tribe, pastures – and (rather artificially) distributes the list of evils among them.

33·1

The ruling will be so implemented as by the statutes of the first
    existence,
by action most just both for the wrongful one and as regards the
    righteous
and for him whose false and straight deeds are put in the balance.

2

He that does evil to the wrongful one, whether by word or
    thought
or hands, or instructs his comrade in goodness,
such men will be prompt to His will, in the Mindful Lord's
    favour.

3

He that is best to the righteous one, whether with clan or village
or tribe, Lord, or by tending the cow with care,
will be in the pasture of Right and Good Thought.

4

I that by worship will seek to keep from Thee, Mindful One,
    disregard and bad thought
and the clan's arrogance and the village's closest neighbour,
    Wrong,
and the detractors in the tribe, and from the cow's pasture the
    worst counsellor,

(5) At the end of life's journey, in an old age in which Good Thought has established its control, on that path that leads direct from and to Right and the Mindful Lord, Zoroaster will call upon *Sraoša* (literally Hearkening, Obedience), the embodiment of his own devotion to the Mindful One, which is supreme (literally 'all-greatest'; that is, probably, surpassing anyone else's), to testify for him and provide the reward that he deserves for it (cf. 43. 12).

(6) In short, he is an unimpeachable minister (*zaotar-*, the traditional word for the priest who poured out the libation). His impulses are of the best, and once again their pastoral dimension is not to be forgotten. (It is not clear whether this refers strictly to the pasture of animals or has a wider metaphorical reference to the guidance of the human community.) With these credentials he desires to meet and confer with the Mindful Lord face to face.

(7) The meeting is now solicited through the format of a traditional invocational prayer for the god or gods to come into the worshipper's presence. At a conventional ceremony the patron of the sacrifice would hope for their coming to receive the gifts offered; Zoroaster has a higher claim on their attention on account of his righteousness and good thought. Let us all make manifest these oblations that will attract the entities invoked. For the kind of offerings envisaged compare stanza 14.

(8) Let the Mindful One take note of Zoroaster's virtuous endeavours, of how he worships him as a kindred spirit and composes worthy hymns to him. Let him reward his priest-poet with those blessings that are in his gift from the original dispensation: continuing life (literally 'not dying'), health, and vitality.

5

I that will invoke (my) all-surpassing compliance to Thee at the
journey's end[12]
after achieving long life, the realm of Good Thought,
the paths that lead straight from Right, on which the Mindful
Lord dwells,

6

I that minister straight in accord with right: from this my best
will I desire,
with that mind by which one takes it in mind to do pastoral works
I long, Mindful Lord, to see Thee and confer with Thee.

7

Come to me, Best ones, come, Mindful One, in Thine own
person and confidently[13]
with Right and Good Thought, for which I am renowned above
the sacrifice-patrons:
let there be seen among us manifest reverential offerings.

8

Take note of my endeavours that I will prosecute with good
thought,
Your follower's worship, Mindful One, or my words of praise
in accord with Right.
Continuing life was created as Your portion, and health with
vitality.

---

[12] Literally 'at the unharnessing'.
[13] Or 'visibly'.

(9) When Zoroaster is uncertain what course of action to take, there takes place (as in 31. 12) a tussle between two inner voices. These are the two rival intents described in *Yasna* 30 and 45. 2, the good one and the bad, but they are identified here only by the allusion to one of them bringing increase through Right. This is the one that Zoroaster wants to make his own; 'let it be brought Thee' (literally 'let one bring Thee') continues the language of conventional divine service and offerings. In adopting the good intent and making it an offering, Zoroaster shows a soul in accord with the Mindful Lord's, and this is an earnest of their enduring association.

(10) All who have lived good lives in the past, are living them now, or will do so in the future, deserve a place in the Mindful Lord's favour. By taking them to himself, with their good thought and adherence to Right, he can increase his own being and extend his sway as much as he wishes.

(11) Zoroaster now appeals in traditional prayer form to the whole collectivity of divine beings. The conventional expressions 'hear me, have mercy upon me' are given an individual turn by the specification 'at the allocation of whatever it may be', that is, when his life is judged.

(12) He continues with a development of the idea in stanza 10 that the Mindful Lord is himself augmented and fortified by his worshipper's qualities. The indeterminate 'allocation' of the previous stanza is now qualified as a 'good' dispensation: Zoroaster hopes that it will be good in his case, and that his adherence to the Positive Will in his moral decisions will lead the Mindful Lord to be prompt in enacting the allocation.

9

Let that intent, Mindful One, of the two rival ones, the one that
   brings increase through right
with well-being, be brought Thee with best thought when I am
   uncertain;
the fellowship of those two is established, whose souls agree.

10

All those good lives that have been and those that are
and those, Mindful One, that shall come to be, give them shares
   in Thy favour;
grow in substance with Good Thought, Dominion, and Right as
   Thou wilt.

11

Thou who art the strongest Lord and the Mindful One, and
   (Thou) also Piety,
and Right that promotes its flock, and Good Thought, and
   Dominion,
hear me, have mercy on me at the dispensation of whatever it
   may be.

12

Come forth to me, Lord, through (my) piety assume strength,
through (my) most bounteous will, Mindful One, promptness
   with good dispensation,
through (my) right, powerful force, through (my) good thought,
   respect.

(13) To assist him in his endeavours, he prays to see the several facets of temporal power that are the reward of good thought; and he prays to Piety (the divine projection of his own piety) to keep his religious conceptions on the true course.

(14) Following a traditional practice, the priest-poet names himself at the end of his song. This is not a hymn accompanying an actual ritual of dedication, but it shows the influence of such hymns (stanzas 6, 7, 11), and now Zoroaster identifies his own offering, not a material but a spiritual one. As people dedicate the first and best specimens of their produce to the gods, so he dedicates the 'firstness' of his good thought, speech, and action, as well as the devotion of which he spoke in stanza 5, and such authority or empowerment as he has achieved or hopes yet to achieve.

13

For (my) support, O Far-seeing one, show me the *virtues* that are
    Yours,
those of dominion, Lord, which are the reward of good thought;
O bounteous Piety and Right, teach (me) moral principles.

14

As offering, Zarathushtra dedicates his own body's energy
to the Mindful One and Right, the prime of his good thought
and deed and utterance, his compliance and authority.

YASNA 34

This poem has some thematic similarities with the previous one, but here there is more reference to Zoroaster's community, and its conflicts with the enemy appear in the background.

The first stanzas take up the idea at the end of *Yasna* 33, that the worshipper's pious thought, speech, and action are his offering to the Mindful Lord. (1) From such offerings the Lord builds up his stock of those desirable qualities, continuing life and health in the way of Right, that are his to bestow on deserving mortals. We offer these to Thee, Lord – and there are many of us! (2) But it is one man, Zoroaster himself, who makes this dedication in the presence of his whole 'flock' through his songs of praise. (3) He commends the whole flock, which has been raised on the fodder of good thought, to the Mindful Lord and to Right. Its collective worth assures the benefit sought by the one who so generously offers it.[14]

(4) They pray for the Lord's powerful fire, which will help their cause and harm the enemy's. If, as other passages would suggest, this is the fire that is instrumental in the allocation of their deserts to the good and the bad after death, the present prayer will mean, 'we look forward to meeting this test and seeing our foes finally undone by it'.

---

[14] This stanza is patterned on the model of a sacrificial ritual in which a wealthy patron offers up a quantity of animals to the gods who have provided for their nurture, in the expectation of benefit commensurate with his generosity.

34.1

The deed, the word, the worship through which Thou assumest
for Thyself
continuing life and Right, Mindful One, and the domain of health,
of these is offering made Thee, Lord, by us in our great numbers.

2

They are all dedicated to Thee by the thought and from the good
intent
and by the deed of a liberal man, whose soul accords with Right,
in Your follower's hymn before his flock, Mindful One, with
songs of praise.

3

As Thy oblation, Lord, and Right's, we will reverently give
into Thy sway all our living bodies, that Ye have nurtured with
good thought;
for it is established by (You) all, Mindful One, that the munificent
giver is furthered among Your followers.

4

We wish for Thy fire, Lord, which is mighty through Right,
very potent and strong, to be present as a manifest help to Thy
supporter,
but to Thy foe, Mindful One, a visible hurt by main force.

(5) Zoroaster asks the three principal entities about the extent of their power to protect him, their poor dependant who is at their disposal. They answer that they have pronounced him worthier than all those who harass his community, both the human marauders and the gods they worship. This is not a guarantee of his safety, but the implication is that the divine Lords will give him their best support.

(6) If that is really so, he continues, let them demonstrate it in every situation as he goes through the ups and downs of life. Then, when he goes to meet them with worship and praise, he will do so all the more joyfully.

(7) We could wish that the Mindful Lord had a whole regiment of agents, trained in the principles laid down by Good Thought and in the consequences of following or neglecting them, to combat all the contrarieties of life. But where are they? Zoroaster knows only the Mindful One himself and his immediate associates; so let them give us the protection we need against the wrongful.

(8) We are fearful of them because of the way they have behaved in the past, with their aggressive actions that threatened the welfare of many in the region. They repudiated the Mindful One's law and failed to think on Right, and Good Thought removed itself far from them.

5

What is Your power, what Your ability for action, Mindful One,
    as I am in Your hands,[15]
with Right and Good Thought to protect Your poor dependant?
'We have declared you beyond all predators,[16] both Daevas and
    mortals.'

6

If Ye are truly thus, Mindful One with Right and Good Thought,
then prove that to me through all the vicissitudes of this life,
so that I may approach You the more gladly with worship and
    praise.

7

Where are Thy zealous ones, Mindful One, who by acquiring
    Good Thought's
edicts and inheritance can make even misfortunes, even sorrows
    innocuous?
I know none such other than You, with Right; so protect us!

8

For they intimidate us by those actions of theirs in which there
    was previously danger to many,
as a strong man does a weaker one, in hostility to Thy law,
    Mindful One;
from those who were not thinking on Right, Good Thought was
    far away.

[15] Emended reading; the transmitted text has the senseless phrase 'or the way I sleep'.
[16] See note on 28. 5.

(9) That is what happens when perpetrators of bad acts reject the Zoroastrian's piety because they are lacking in Good Thought: it and its companion Right distance themselves as far from them as those marauders that instigate evil (stanza 5) are removed from us (by our rejection of them).

(10) Anyone wise will advise holding firm to the course of action that springs from good thought; holding firm to Piety, which produces and abides with Right; holding firm to the whole set of virtues that belong in the Mindful Lord's sphere.

(11) Good thought and piety are essential to the Mindful Lord's strength against the enemy. Where Good Thought's wisdom prevails, he feeds on continuing life and health (compare stanza 1); Piety and Right build up his vitality. Thus he takes on the aspect of a well-nourished, formidable warrior, at the sight of whom the enemy quails.

(12) But Zoroaster desires more detailed guidance on how the Mindful Lord wishes to be worshipped and praised, and on how the rewards for following his rules (and the punishments for violating them) will be assigned. Let the Lord proclaim these things, and teach us exactly how to follow the recommended path of good thought.

9

Those who abandon the bounteous piety esteemed of Thy adept,
  Mindful One,
the evil-doers, from their failure to acquire Good Thought,
from them it will retreat a great distance with Right, as far as the
  savage predators do from us. [17]

10

The wise man says seize hold of this Good Thought's actions
and of bounteous Piety, knowing her the creator and companion
  of Right,
and of all those *excellences*, Mindful Lord, that are in Thy domain.

11

Thou hast both health for nourishment and continuing life.
Through the wisdom of Good Thought Piety together with Right
  increases
(Thy) vitality and might; with (all) these, Mindful One, Thou
  puttest the enemy in fear.

12

What is Thy rule, what dost Thou wish, what of praise, or what
  of worship?
Tell for our hearing, Mindful One, how the rewards of (Thy)
  rulings might be distributed;
teach us with Right the paths of Good Thought that are well to
  travel:

---

[17] Or according to a variant reading, 'from it'.

(13) It is a well-paved path on which one may walk without stumbling. On this road the moral perceptions of the Promoters, that is, those committed adherents of the faith whose mission is to strengthen it and make the world better, move forward, following the track laid down by Good Thought. It leads to the reward that the Mindful Lord has appointed for the good. And when that reward is given, it turns out to be wisdom itself, what the Mindful Lord personifies. (14) For this is the prize to be won by the people of the pastoral community, if they put good thought into practice: enlightenment in the wisdom that enables communities to prosper.

(15) So Zoroaster repeats his appeal to the Mindful Lord (not forgetting Good Thought and Right) to instruct him, in return for his hymn of praise, in the best ways of acting and winning repute. Zoroaster has a vision of a new world, restored to its pristine perfection: let the Mindful Lord, by exercising his sway, bring it about.

13

that road, Lord, of which Thou tellest me, the one of Good
  Thought,
the well-paved one on which the Promoters' moral selves[18] set
  forth with Right itself
to the reward Ye assigned to well-doers, Mindful One, of which
  Thou art the gift.

14

For this, Mindful One, is the prize Ye will bestow on material
  life
from the enactment of good thought by all those in the community
  of the milch cow:
Your enlightenment, Lord, in the wisdom that promotes com-
  munities with Right.

15

Mindful One, tell me the best things to be known for and to do,
those things, Thou with Good Thought and with Right, in return
  for my hymn of praise;
through Your dominion, Lord, make real the existence that is
  splendid in my desiring.

[18] 'Promoters' is my translation of *saošyantō*; see p. 15.

YASNA 43

This hymn, addressed to the Mindful Lord almost through-out, combines praise of his beneficence with expressions of Zoroaster's piety and aspirations.

(1) Different people want different things, and so far as Zoroaster is concerned, the Mindful Lord may give any of them what they want, at his pleasure; but what he himself wants is the strength and energy to hold firm to Right, and the life governed by good thought. He deserves them as 'rewards for wealth', or perhaps rather 'in exchange for wealth': not returns for wealth that he has expended, but compensations for the wealth that has been denied him.

(2) A man who enjoys material well-being may compound it by acquiring, and maintaining throughout his life, an understand-ing of how good thought can transform everything for the better, a property conferred on it by the Mindful Lord and Right.

(3) But even better than the best is appropriate as reward for whoever could teach us the most direct path to material and spiritual advancement, that upward path towards the abode of the Mindful One. Such a man would be a faithful follower of the Lord, with the same generosity of spirit, and of some standing in society by virtue of his birth.

(4) The generosity of the Lord, who dispenses their various deserts to good and bad through the fire of Right, will be proved when he grants Zoroaster the power of good thought that brings those benefits.

43.1

To anyone whose wishes he grants at all
may the Mindful Lord, ruling at will, grant his wishes.
Vitality and strength are what I wish to attend me
for taking hold of Right – grant me that, O Piety –
(those) compensations for wealth, (and) the life of good thought.

2

But best of all could a man
add well-being to well-being for himself
by understanding through Thy most bounteous will, Mindful
One,
the transforming powers of good thought that Thou hast created
with Right,
all his days as he enjoys long life.

3

But may that man attain yet better than the good,
who should teach us the straight paths of advancement
in this material existence and that of thought,
the true *gradients* that the Lord inhabits:
a zealous follower of Thine, Mindful One, well-born, bounteous.

4

I will think Thee bold and bounteous, Mindful One,
when by that hand, in which Thou holdest those
rewards that Thou didst set for the wrongful one and the righteous
through the heat of Thy fire that Right makes mighty,
the force of good thought comes to me.

(5) But there is already much evidence of his generosity, and for the remainder of the poem each pair of stanzas starts from the same affirmation, 'Bounteous I think Thee, Mindful Lord,' followed by a reason. (But the formula soon becomes mechanical, and its relationship to what follows in each case is not easy to see.) Zoroaster begins by again (as in 31. 8) picturing the Mindful One at the beginning of creation, when he established the system of rewarding people according to their merits when they come into the final straight on the racecourse of life.

(6) There they learn their fates from Piety and Good Thought, who can testify to the degree of piety and good thought that those arriving have shown in their lives. The Mindful Lord judges them wisely and accurately, and none can deceive him.

(7) As an occasion for affirming his own faith, Zoroaster imagines himself being questioned by a well-disposed enquirer. A standard enquiry about someone's identity was 'who are you, and whose (son)?' Here the 'whose?' is probably to be understood in a more general sense, so that if Zoroaster had answered it explicitly, the answer would have been 'the Mindful Lord's'. (8) In answer to the enquirer Zoroaster proudly declares his name and his moral orientation. His aims are to oppose the wrongful and support the righteous, in the hope of obtaining the good offices of 'Him who rules at will' (the title adapted from stanza 1, with no special point here) and of enjoying them for as long as he goes on praising him, by which he no doubt intends 'all my life'. In the last line he switches from third to second person as he resumes his address to the Mindful Lord.

5

Bounteous I think Thee, Mindful Lord,
when I see Thee at the first in the genesis of the world,
when Thou didst set wages for actions and for speech:
evil for the evil one, a good reward for the good
by Thy genius, at the last bend of creation.[1]

6

At that bend where Thou comest with Thy bounteous will
mindful in dominion, there, with Good Thought
by whose actions the flock prospers with Right,
Piety announces to them the verdicts
of Thy wisdom, which[2] no one deceives.

7

Bounteous I think Thee, Mindful Lord,
when one approaches me with good thought
and asks me, 'Who art thou? Whose art thou?
How mightest thou take a day (for me) to ask teaching
about thy flock and thyself?'

8

To him I say in the first place, 'Zarathushtra am I:
may I be in reality, as I would wish, the bane of the wrongful one
and to the righteous a strong support,
so I may obtain the offices of Him who rules at will
as long as I am praising and hymning Thee, Mindful One.'

---

[1] Racecourse metaphor.
[2] Or '(Thou) whom'.

(9) The same switch takes place at once in the reply to the enquirer's next question. The Mindful Lord's fire is identified as the focus of Zoroaster's devotion; he may be thinking both of the sacred altar fire and of the fire which he mentions elsewhere in connection with the judgment of mortals and dispensation of their deserts. This fire is closely associated with Right (31. 3, 34. 4, 43. 4), and so here the service of the fire is equated with reverence of Right.

(10) With his piety to support his prayer, Zoroaster asks for Right to be revealed to him, and declares himself ready to answer more questions; the Mindful One's questions will be (for his poetic purpose) equivalent to those asked by the enquirer of the earlier stanzas. The questioning will give the pious prophet the opportunity to broadcast his convictions and so strengthen the Mindful One.

(11) From here on, although 'Bounteous I think Thee . . . ' continues to be followed with 'when one attends me . . . ', this person no longer plays a role. It is all between Zoroaster and the Mindful Lord. Zoroaster has come to rely on his guidance to do what is right, instead of following what mortals say. (12) The guidance is to take his lessons from Right. This Zoroaster will be sure to do in good time, before that day when Compliance will come, with his attendant Reward, to identify those who have honoured him and who deserve to be rewarded (cf. 33. 5).

9

Bounteous I think Thee, Mindful Lord,
when one approaches me with good thought,
(and) at his question, 'Whom dost thou wish to serve?'
I declare, Thy fire; the tribute of reverence
of Right, so far as I can, I shall hold in mind.

10

Show me Thou Right, that one I constantly invoke –
in company with Piety I have started towards it –
and ask us what Thou hast to ask us
(for the question asked by Thee is like that of the *proselytes*),[3]
so that one might be enabled to make Thee potent and strong.

11

Bounteous I think Thee, Mindful Lord,
when one approaches me with good thought,
as I am learning by Your utterances first of all –
(for) trust in mortals reveals itself to me as pain and grief –
to do that which Ye tell me is best;

12

and when in Thy providence Thou tellest me, 'Go to Right',
Thou givest me advice that will not go unheeded,
to start out before there comes to me
Compliance accompanied by Reward that confers riches,
who should distribute the two parties' rewards in the allocation
    of strength.

---

[3] *Proselytes* restored by conjecture.

(13) It is good when well-disposed people take note of the good things that Zoroaster does from his desire for the reward which, as he has heard (from the divine voice), the Mindful Lord has in his gift: the long life. The Lord (who rules at will, as has been mentioned) is free to give it or withhold it. (14) But an affluent man might be expected to share his possessions with his friend, and so may the Mindful One give his friend Zoroaster his providential support, who deserves it because he has followed Right, so that in alliance with the whole army of the faithful he can drive away their detractors.

(15) The idea of this stanza is similar to that of stanza 11: Zoroaster derives what he has to say from silent meditation (in which he hears the Mindful Lord's words), not from listening to others, whose discourses (poems?) often express the viewpoint of the wrongful.

(16) Naming himself again at the end of the poem, the prophet affirms his commitment to the Bounteous Will that urges a man to choose the better courses of action. He prays to see Right and Piety flourishing in the world about him, coupled with Dominion, in other words prevailing and able to operate unhindered; and to receive from Piety (as in stanza 1) the reward for what he has done under Good Thought's guidance.

13

Bounteous I think Thee, Mindful Lord,
when one approaches me with good thought
to take note of the endeavours of this desire Ye have given me
for the long life, to which no one forces You to accede,
a desirable commodity said to lie in Thy domain.

14

What a man of means, possessing it himself, would offer a friend,
give me, Mindful One: Thy providential support,
which under Thy dominion is attained in accord with Right,
to start out and drive off the detractors of Thy law
in concert with all those who mind Thy prescripts.

15

Bounteous I think Thee, Mindful Lord,
when one approaches me with good thought:
silent meditation teaches me the best things to say.
Let a man not be one to gratify the many wrongful:
they have declared all the righteous their enemies.

16

O Lord, this Zarathushtra chooses that will,
whichever, Mindful One, is Thy most bounteous one.
May Right be there in bodily form, vigorously strong;
may Piety be there in sight of the sun with Dominion;
may she grant reward on account of actions with Good Thought.

YASNA 44

This poem of just 100 lines, the longest in the collection and perhaps the finest, stands exactly in the middle of the series. It is a cardinal document for the beginnings of Zoroastrianism, giving us a vivid picture of its precarious foothold among a small body of supporters and the prophet's efforts to gain converts.

Formally the poem consists of a series of questions to the Mindful Lord, every stanza but the last beginning with the same line. We have seen something similar on a small scale in 31. 14–16. The 'I ask Thee' formula and the raising of cosmological issues in question form are also found in the Rigveda and appear to have been traditional motifs. The questions about the ordering of the physical cosmos in stanzas 3–5 are the purest echoes of this tradition. For the rest, Zoroaster's usual preoccupations prevail: how one should live, how the good religion is to be promoted and triumph over the adherents of Wrong, and how at present the prophet lives in uncertain and unsatisfactory circumstances.

(1) The first question is the general one of how the Mindful Lord ought to be worshipped, which amounts to asking what are the basic principles of the religion. Zoroaster is the Mindful One's friend and deserves his confidence. He and his followers need this advice because they need to be on good terms with Right, to secure its presence and that of Good Thought among them.

(2) The aim is to bring the world into the best possible state. How is the well-intentioned man to set about mending it and consolidating the improvement? For this is the kind of man who is needed to cure the sickness of existence as an ally of the Mindful Lord: outgoing, generous, guided by Right, conscious of the outcomes awaiting everyone in accordance with their conduct.

44.1

This I ask Thee, tell me straight, Lord,
(I ask) out of reverence, how Your kind is to be revered:
Mindful One, I hope one like Thee may declare it to a friend
    such as me.
We (worshippers) have friendly relations to maintain with Right,
so that it will come to us with Good Thought.

2

This I ask Thee, tell me straight, Lord:
how can the best existence's beginning
be furthered by the man of good will who is to take those things
    forward?
For it is such a man, liberal with Right, observing the outcome
    for all,
who by his intent is a healer of existence, an ally, Mindful One.

(3–5) Who gave birth to Right in the first place? The question about origins leads Zoroaster into the more general and more traditional series of questions about the cosmos and who created it and controls it. In the middle of these questions he works in one about Good Thought, to complement the initial one about Right. We would guess that his answer to all these questions would have been 'the Mindful Lord', but he leaves them open.

(6) Two further favourite concepts are now brought in, piety and dominion. Piety, the proper attitude of mind, when expressed in action, confirms Right and widens the Mindful Lord's dominion. But if that is so, what are we to make of the unhappy situation of the cow (as depicted in *Yasna* 29)? Who was she made for: the stock-raiser and the herdsman (as the Mindful One himself declared in 29. 6), or those who claim her for sacrifice?

3

This I ask Thee, tell me straight, Lord:
who was the father-begetter of Right in the beginning?
Who set the path of the sun and stars?
Who is it through whom the moon waxes or wanes?
These things, Mindful One, I desire to know, and others besides.

4

This I ask Thee, tell me straight, Lord:
who held the earth from beneath, and the heavens
from falling down? Who the waters and plants?
Who yoked the wind's and the clouds' swift pair?
Who is the creator, Mindful One, of Good Thought?

5

This I ask Thee, tell me straight, Lord:
what skilful artificer made the light and the darkness?
What skilful artificer made sleep and waking?
Who is it through whom there are morning, noon, and eve,
that make the prudent man mindful of his endeavour?

6

This I ask Thee, tell me straight, Lord:
if these propositions are true,
that Piety in action confirms Right
and assigns dominion to Thee together with Good Thought,
for what (class of) people didst Thou fashion the gladdening
    milch cow?

(7) Piety and dominion are now added to the list of those whose origins are asked about. The question about the son's respect for his father does not make an obvious sequel, but Zoroaster may be thinking of the principle of obedience or compliance (*sraoša-*), which is important in connection with moral and religious instruction, and the father–son relationship may stand symbolically for that between teacher and disciple (cf. 45. 11), or between the Mindful Lord and his whole creation. – All these questions, Zoroaster affirms, are designed to further the recognition of the Mindful One as ordainer of all things through his bounteous will.

(8) Zoroaster now narrows the focus to his personal aspirations. He is anxious to follow the guidance of the Mindful Lord and his two associates, Right and Good Thought; he makes consultation with Good Thought, and Right presides over the correct perceptions concerning the way of existence. What are the good ends that his soul can expect to attain?

(9) And can he hope for his religion to be taken up and set on a firm footing by someone with temporal power?

7

This I ask Thee, tell me straight, Lord:
who fashions the piety that we esteem together with dominion?
Who by his wisdom made the son respectful to the father?
I with these questions am providently promoting Thee, Mindful
   One,
the ordainer of all things through Thy bounteous will.

8

This I ask Thee, tell me straight, Lord,
so I may take Thy instruction to heart, Mindful One,
and the words spoken by Good Thought that I obtain in consul-
   tation,
and those fitly to be apprehended through Right about existence:
to what good destinations will my soul journey?

9

This I ask Thee, tell me straight, Lord:
the religion of mine that I am to perfect,
how might the master of a beneficent dominion proclaim it for
   me
with righteous rule, a very potent follower of Thine, Mindful
   One,
abiding with Right and Good Thought?

(10) It is the best religion there is; he prays that its practice, and the influence of Right, will benefit his community; but have they got the right conception of it, and do they speak and act in accordance with true piety? The prophet has his pure vision, but what effect it will have lies in the Mindful One's hands.

(11) When Zoroaster teaches his religion to others, how can he imbue them with the requisite piety? They are the ones he relies on, the first converts to his new religion; he looks askance at everybody else.

(12) He questions people about their beliefs, but he cannot be sure of the sincerity of their responses. Which of them is genuinely on the side of Right? Which is a genuine supporter, and which is really an opponent? The Lord replies: the enemy is the one who deliberately opposes and obstructs the progress that Zoroaster makes in promoting the Mindful One.

(13) Zoroaster continues: how can we at least expel Wrong from our own party and confine it to the opposition, those irredeemably unwilling to listen to instruction, who make no effort to associate themselves with Right and never ask themselves what Good Thought would recommend?

10

This I ask Thee, tell me straight, Lord:
that religion which is the best in existence —
may it promote my flock in union with Right —
do they with pious words and deed have a true conception of it?
My insight is Thine to command at Thy discretion, Mindful One.

11

This I ask Thee, tell me straight, Lord:
how might piety spread to those
to whom Thy religion, Mindful One, goes forth?
I with them am the first to *find my way* to Thee:
all others I regard with hostile spirit.

12

This I ask Thee, tell me straight, Lord:
who is righteous or wrongful of those I question?
Which is my enemy, this one or that one?
'The wrongful one who takes pleasure in attacking thy gains,
he it is, not the other, who thinks as an enemy.'

13

This I ask Thee, tell me straight, Lord:
how are we to drive Wrong out from ourselves
down upon those who, being full of non-compliance,
do not strive for the companionship of Right
and have not had the pleasure of consulting Good Thought?

(14) How might we go further and defeat Wrong altogether by means of the 'mantras' of the Mindful Lord's edict, that is, by means of Zoroaster's formulations of the Lord's instruction; deal the adherents of Wrong a crushing blow, and afflict them with pain and grief?

(15) Zoroaster's language has by this stage become quite bellicose, as if he were looking forward not just to a conflict of religions but to actual fighting. Now he speaks of hostile armies coming together in a battle over the principles that the Mindful Lord would uphold. But which will prevail? There is a suggestion that Zoroaster himself may be in danger and need protection.

(16) Who is the human champion, dedicated to following the Mindful One's injunctions, who will protect everyone in the community? Zoroaster longs for a clear and manifest answer to his needs, a man with the will and capability to put the world to rights. Let the Lord assign this role to someone with the power and authority to sort things out, and let this man, whoever it may be, be led by good thought to *sraoša-*, consistent obedience or hearkening to the Mindful Lord.

(17) In short, how is Zoroaster to fulfil his ambition of a secure relationship with the higher entities (cf. stanza 1)? How is he to make his voice effective, as he diligently pursues his goal of continued life and health by formulating in verse the requirements of Right?

14

This I ask Thee, tell me straight, Lord:
how might I give Wrong into the hands of Right
to destroy her with the prescripts of Thy law,
to deliver a crushing blow on the wrongful,
to bring pains upon them, Mindful One, and harassments?

15

This I ask Thee, tell me straight, Lord:
if Thou hast this power with Right, to protect me
when the two hostile armies meet
on those terms which Thou, Mindful One, wouldst uphold,
where between the two and to whom dost Thou give the victory?

16

This I ask Thee, tell me straight, Lord:
who is the victorious one to protect with Thy law (all) who
    exist —
let me be given clarity — the healer of the world? Assign his role,
and let Compliance come to him with Good Thought,
Mindful One, to whom Thou wilt soever.

17

This I ask Thee, tell me straight, Lord:
how am I to journey in accord with You towards my goal
of attachment to You, and make my voice effective
in working for union with health and continuing life
by means of that prescript which cleaves to Right?

(18) This stanza develops the same idea. How is he to earn that boon of life and health, now represented as a reward that the Mindful Lord (who enjoys those properties himself) has promised him? The unexpected intrusion of 'ten mares with stallion and a camel' assimilates the situation to that of the priest-poet who, like the Vedic Rishi, expects and receives substantial rewards of livestock from his patron. Probably Zoroaster has no actual expectation of these animals from anyone, but uses them as a symbol of the highest level of reward.

(19) If the Mindful Lord does not give the reward that Zoroaster has earned, despite having awarded the same boons to himself, he is like a mortal patron who keeps for himself what he has promised to his praise-poet. Such a man will surely be punished hereafter.

(20) Zoroaster's campaign certainly deserves the Mindful Lord's support. After all, he cannot say that the religion of the traditional gods is acceptable, considering the sufferings of the cow at the hands of the various priestly orders, sufferings that prompt her soul to such laments as were portrayed in *Yasna* 29. These rites conflict with the proper development of pastoralism, which is what Right requires.

18

This I ask Thee, tell me straight, Lord:
how am I to earn that reward with Right —
the ten mares with stallion, and the camel —
which was promised me, Mindful One, with health
and continuing life, even as Thou takest these for Thyself?

19

This I ask Thee, tell me straight, Lord:
he that does not give that reward to one who earns it,
the man who awards it to himself when it has been promised,
what punishment for that will strike him at the first?
For I know the one that will strike him at the last.

20

What, Mindful One, has the Daevas' dominion been good —
that is what I ask — they that *blaspheme* for the sake of those
with whom the Karpan and the Usij subject the cow to violence
and (to all the ills) that the Kavi makes her lament to her soul?[4]
They do not care for her so as to promote the pasture with Right.

---

4 Those that she complains of in 29. 1.

YASNA 45

This poem is related to *Yasna* 30. As there, Zoroaster addresses a congregation of people who have become interested in his discourses and have gathered from several quarters to hear another one. As in *Yasna* 43 and 44, the device of a repeated refrain is used to thread a series of stanzas together: the first six all begin with the phrase 'I will tell forth'.

(1) Let the hearers listen well and take his message to heart. Those who (first) propagated the old religion were responsible for corrupting the pristine perfection of life by leading people along the wrong path (cf. 30. 6). This must not be allowed to happen a second time.

(2) Again as in *Yasna* 30, Zoroaster starts from the doctrine (here treated as if already familiar) of the two contrasted Wills or Mentalities that came into being at the beginning of the world. The total antithesis between them is expressed in a declaration made by the Positive Will in which he dissociates himself entirely from the Negative one.

(3) Zoroaster proposes to tell about the world's beginning, literally its 'first (thing)'. He actually means what he has just told us in the previous stanza; we might have expected this announcement to come first. As it is, the intention is to explain how he knows what the Positive Will said at the beginning. The Mindful Lord has told him of it. His 'mantra' or prescript, his poetic statement of what the Lord has communicated to him, is to be taken as a guide on how to live. Those who fail to follow it will be sorry at the last.

45·1

I will tell forth – now listen ye, now hear ye,
you proselytes from near and from far;
now all take it to heart, for it is clear.
May the false teacher not be ruining the world a second time
with his bad option, the wrongful one cloaked in his prating.

2

I will tell forth the two Wills at the world's beginning,
of whom the Bounteous one speaks thus to the Hostile one:
'Neither our thoughts, nor our pronouncements, nor our intel-
    lects,
nor our choices, nor our words, nor our deeds,
nor our moralities, nor our souls, are in accord.'

3

I will tell forth this world's beginning,
as the Mindful Lord told me of it from His knowledge.
Those of you who do not act on this prescript
in the way that I conceive and speak it,
for them 'Woe!' will be their worldly life's end.

(4) After telling of the world's First (thing, neuter), Zoroaster will now tell of its Best (one, masculine). This again refers back to stanza 2, for the Best One must be identified as the Positive Will; there is no other plausible candidate, given that he was created by the Mindful Lord and is the father of Good Thought and Piety. Good Thought prompts people to virtuous actions, and so does Piety. We have thus a causal hierarchy, partly expressed in genealogical terms: the Mindful Lord > the Positive Will > Good Thought and Piety > good actions. The Mindful Lord, at the top of the chain, observes all that goes on and cannot be deluded. (So beware, because he observes your conduct too and controls the outcome.)

(5) Zoroaster repeats that his message comes from the Mindful Lord. It is the best of messages to listen to and obey; those who do so will attain the goal of continuing life and health. The essence of the message is that the all-observant Lord takes note when people translate good thought into good action, and will reward them.

(6) After the First (stanza 3) and the Best (stanza 4), now Zoroaster will tell of the Greatest: the Mindful Lord himself, the benefactor of all who exist. Let him hear the praise-song, together with its other principal honorand, the Positive Will, for it is a well-considered composition: in formulating it Zoroaster has sought guidance from Good Thought. And let him continue to instruct him in the best lessons to pass on to his audiences.

(7) He is not only the benefactor of those currently alive, for the blessings he offers are available equally to the righteous who are no longer on earth or are yet to be born: to those no longer on earth, because their souls enjoy a form of continuing life (to the chagrin of the wrongful) in a realm which is – like the Positive Will, etc. (stanza 4) – the creation of the Mindful One.

4

I will tell forth this world's Best One
in accord with Right; the Mindful One who made him knows
　　him,
(him) the father of Good Thought that stimulates to action;[5]
and he has a daughter who does good deeds, Piety.
There is no deceiving the all-observant Lord.

5

I will tell forth what the most Bounteous One tells me,
the word that is best for mortals to hear.
Whatever people comply with it for me
will attain health and continuing life:
enactments of good thought make the Lord mindful.

6

I will tell forth the Greatest One of all,
praising with Right Him who is a benefactor (of all) who are:
with the Bounteous Will let the Mindful Lord hear.
Let Him in whose lauding I have consulted with Good Thought
by His sapience teach me the best lessons.

7

The Caring One whose strengthening all may set in train,
those living, and who have been, and who will come to be –
(for) the righteous man's soul is active in continued life
and in vitality, which is vexation to the men of Wrong;
of those realms too the Mindful Lord is the creator –

---

[5] In 31. 8 Mazdā himself is the father of Good Thought. But here the reference is to the
Bounteous Will.

(8) This beneficent deity Zoroaster sees in his mind's eye while in the process of composing a hymn that will engage his attention: the picture forms as he contemplates the workings of the Good Will as manifested in the words and deeds of those motivated by him. The Mindful Lord is recognized behind all this, and it is to him that the singer's praises are offered on behalf of the group.

(9) The hymn aims also to make him (and his associate, Good Thought) pleased with the worshippers, since he exercises his power with intelligent discrimination and brings fortune or misfortune on us at his discretion. May he see to it that we are well acquainted with good thought and endowed with the strength and vigour to conduct our affairs in a good way, to the benefit (and not the disruption) of the pastoral economy.

(10) And thirdly the hymn, as a pious act of worship, seeks to magnify him, the Lord whom Zoroaster not only sees in his mind's eye but hears in his soul. When he, together with Right and Good Thought, decides that someone is worthy of it, they put within his reach those two desirable pairs: continuing life and health, strength and vitality.

(11) Whoever follows the lead of Zoroaster and his followers and is not cowed by the hostility of those who uphold the old religion, but opposes all who do not show the proper attitude towards the Mindful One, counts as the ally and brother, or (if senior enough) as the father, of the 'Promoter householder' who is the pillar of the movement, the stock-farmer who has determined to support it. The faithful are a family.

8

Him, seeking to envelop Him in our reverent praises,
I have just now discerned in my eye,
of the Good Will's deed and utterance
apprised with Right, Him the Mindful Lord;
for Him we have dedicated laudations in the house of song:

9

seeking (also) to make Him, together with Good Thought,
     pleased with us,
Him who makes our fortune and misfortune at His discretion,
mindful in His dominion: may the Lord make us vigorous
for betterment of our herds and men
from our familiarity with thought that is good through Right:

10

seeking (also) to magnify Him with Piety's acts of worship,
Him that is heard now in my soul, the Mindful Lord.
When with Right and Good Thought He assigns (them) to one,
into his control (then) health and continuing life
they give to be his, (and) strength and vitality.

11

Whoever so follows us in scorning
the Daevas and mortals who scorn Him —
all but that one who is properly disposed towards Him —
he by his liberal morality is the Promoter householder's
ally, brother, or father, O Mindful Lord.

YASNA 46

Here Zoroaster is preoccupied with external circumstances, with his reception among men. There is a shift of perspective in the course of the poem. In the early stanzas the situation is bad: Zoroaster is something of an outcast, and his religion is not flourishing. Later on he appears in a more confident and cheerful mood, able to name and address a series of allies or potential allies.

(1) Where can I find a congenial milieu? At every level of society – clan, village, tribe, province – I feel alienated; the land is ruled by men who practise the old religion and have little sympathy for mine. Evidently the Mindful Lord is not satisfied with me. What must I do to please him?

(2) I lack influence because I lack wealth, I lack a good-sized establishment of livestock and men. I am your friend, Mindful Lord, so help me. Look how little my right-mindedness avails me.

(3) When and where will the good religion take hold? When will its apostles appear, like new days dawning on the world, to preach the word and restore life to what it should be? And in what district will Right and Good Thought establish themselves? Personally I do not need such intermediaries, as I receive my enlightenment directly from the Mindful Lord.

(4) But the prevalence of the infidel with his hostile attitudes makes it impossible for them to achieve a decisive position of influence anywhere. Anyone who can take away a traditionalist's authority, or eliminate him, will make it easier for the true religion to rise like the sun in the sky.

46.1

What land for refuge, where am I to go for refuge?
They set me apart from clan and tribe;
I am not pleased with the communities I consort with,
nor with the region's wrongful masters.
How am I to please Thee, Mindful Lord?

2

I know why I am ineffectual, Mindful One:
because of my poverty in cattle and poverty in men.
I complain to Thee: look to the matter, Lord,
affording support as a friend would to a friend;
behold[6] the potency of thought that is good through Right.

3

When, Mindful One, will those Oxen of Days[7]
set forth on the path of Right to uphold the world
with stouter declarations, the sapient Promoters?
What people will it (Right) come to aid with Good Thought?
For myself I choose Thee, Lord, for direction.

4

But the wrongful one keeps them, Right's draught
oxen, from coming forth in district or region,
abominable as he is, disagreeable in his deeds.
Whoever dispatches him from authority, Mindful One, or from
     life,
will make those oxen advance on the trajectory of enlightenment.

---

[6] Or 'Thou seest'.
[7] Apparently a traditional poetic phrase meaning 'new dawns'.

(5) It may happen that a pious and godly man is obliged by some agreement to receive a ungodly one in his house. (Zoroaster is probably alluding to some actual situation of which we cannot know the details. One might think of an itinerant priest to whom certain households had to provide hospitality.) In such a case he should warn the clan, to avoid it becoming implicated in any blood sacrifice the man performs; or perhaps it is to avoid the man suffering at their hands, when he has protected status.

(6) But if such a man comes uninvited and without a valid claim to hospitality and is received, the host is compromising himself; the house to which he admits such a partnership becomes identified with the metaphorical House of Wrong (stanza 11; 49. 11, 51. 14). For by aiding the wrongful, one becomes wrongful; the righteous should have the righteous as their friends. This is the clear dichotomy that the Mindful Lord made in the beginning.

(7) What defence do I have against the wrongful ones' aggression, Mindful One? I have my devotion to Right, and my knowledge that your fire will separate us from them, consigning us to bliss and them to damnation. But who will protect me here and now? That is what I want you to tell me in support of my religious stance.

5

As for one who on his own authority should take into his house
  one coming
on the basis of a promise or agreements, a man of good birth
living in rectitude, a righteous man (receiving) a follower of
  Wrong,
a man of discrimination, he should inform his clan
to help it[8] escape, Mindful Lord, from bloodshed.

6

But if one who is not wanted should come to him,
it is Wrong's abodes of partnership that he will be entering;
for he is wrongful who is good to the wrongful,
and he is righteous who has a righteous one as his friend,
as Thou didst establish the original moralities, Lord.

7

Whom dost Thou, Mindful One, set as protector for my kind
when the wrongful one seeks to take hold of me for maltreatment,
other than Thy fire and (Good) Thought,
that pair by whose actions Ye nourish Right, Lord?
Tell forth that teaching for my religion.

[8] Or perhaps 'him'.

(8) Where it is my followers who suffer the aggression, may I be kept safe, and may the aggressor suffer such consequences of his actions as will condemn him to a wretched existence, as wretched as may be.

(9) Where am I to find more supporters? Who will be the first (or next) to apprehend what I have discovered, that the Lord of Right is both benevolent and prompt in action? Are my potential converts starting to act on the message of my poetical discourse about the cow (*Yasna* 29)?

(10) Anyone who helps me to get the proper return for my adherence to Right, or to obtain a measure of authority that I can exercise with my good thought, as well as the existing congregation of worshippers with whom I give praise to the Mindful Lord, may be sure of their reward: when we come to the Arbiter's Crossing they will be allowed across with me to the region of bliss.

(11) The Karpan and Kavi priests, on the other hand, by their authority, commit mortals (who at death must answer for their lives) to bad deeds that corrupt our world. When they approach the Crossing, their souls and consciences will vex them, as they realize that it is their fate to remain for ever in the dismal House of Wrong.

8

As for him who is putting my flock to maltreatment,
may harm not reach me from his actions:
may they recoil on him with hostility,
on his person, so as to keep him from good living
and not from bad living – yes, with whatever hostility, Mindful
    One!

9

Who is that zealous one who will be first to recognize
how I *found* Thee *out* as the promptest,
bounteous in action, the Righteous Lord?
What Right said to Thee, what the Maker of the cow to Right,
are they setting that in train for Thee with good thought?

10

The man or woman, Mindful Lord,
who should give me what Thou knowest are the best things in
    this life,
reward for right, authority with good thought,
and those I join for the lauding of Your kind,
with all of them I shall cross the Arbiter's Crossing.

11

The Karpans and Kavis by their authority yoke
the mortal to bad deeds for the ruination of life.
Their own soul and their own morality will torment them
when they come to where the Arbiter's Crossing is,
to lodge for all time in the abode of Wrong.

(12) In the following stanzas Zoroaster refers to a number of notable individuals who have shown themselves to be in the right camp or who may be willing to give him the desired support. Tūra, son of Friya, became a sympathizer together with his family and gave support to the Zoroastrians. The Mindful Lord showed his approval of them by making them right-thinking.

(13) Anyone who has given Zoroaster material help deserves to be celebrated for it and may expect praise in his poems. He counts as a friend of Right and of the Mindful Lord, who rewards him with a life and prospers those in his care.[9]

(14) 'Who, then,' the Mindful Lord asks, 'fulfils these requirements and looks for the fame that you can confer by naming him?' Zoroaster replies that Vishtaaspa does so: a Kavi, but not a typical one, for the Mindful Lord is with him, and he dwells in the Lord's house, where the souls of Right's followers consort with Good Thought and other virtues (49. 10; compare 44. 9, and stanza 16 below). All who dwell in that house Zoroaster will address in favourable terms. (This presumably applies to those addressed in the three following stanzas.)

(15) The Haecataspa Spitāmas must be a branch of the prophet's own family, as he has the same surname.[10] If the grammar is rightly interpreted, they are not yet completely free from the danger of entanglement with the wrongful: they must still make a decisive break with them, and then they must follow the principles of conduct laid down by the Mindful Lord at the beginning.

---

[9] I translate as 'his flock', it being the same word as is used in stanza 12 and elsewhere for the Zoroastrian 'flock', but here it could refer to livestock.
[10] Cf. 53. 3 with note.

12

When He came forth with Right among the famed
kin and descendants of Tūra Friyāna
who promoted Piety's flock with care,
then He brought them into union with Good Thought
to proclaim it for their support, He the Mindful Lord.

13

He who among mortals has gratified Spitāma Zarathushtra
by his concern, that man is worthy of renown.
The Mindful Lord grants him worldly life,
his flock He promotes together with Good Thought;
we apprehend him as Your and Right's good friend.

14

'O Zarathushtra, which righteous one is thy ally
for the great rite? Who wishes for renown?'[11]
He is the Kavi Vishtaaspa, with whom Thou art.
Those whom Thou, Mindful Lord, bringest together in Thy abode
I will invoke with the utterances of good thought.

15

O Haecataspa Spitāmas, I will say to you:
when ye distinguish between the just and the unjust,
by those actions ye shall win yourselves Right.
By the Lord's original ordinances,
*   *   *   *   *[12]

---

[11] The questions seem to be put by the Mindful Lord. For the 'great rite' cf. 29. 11.
[12] Line missing; probably something like 'ye shall be rewarded with bliss'.

(16) Frashaushtra, a man especially close to Zoroaster (28. 8, 49. 8, 51. 17, 53. 2), is also encouraged to go further on the true path that leads to everything desirable, to the place where the Mindful Lord abides. (17) Then Zoroaster will be able to celebrate his and his brother Djāmaaspa's acceptance of the faith in the verses with which he hymns the Lord, who will not fail to recognize their righteousness and give them their due.

(18) Whoever promotes his interests Zoroaster repays as best he can, and whoever shows him hatred he requites with hatred, thus discriminating in the same way as do the Mindful One and Right. (19) To the man who will help him realize his vision of restoring the world to its ideal state, he pledges the most generous reward he can afford: two cows. Besides this prize from the material world, such a man will deserve all the spiritual riches of the world beyond – but those things are in the Mindful Lord's gift.

16

O Frashaushtra son of Hugava, go with those zealous ones
whom we two wish to have their heart's desire
to where Piety is together with Right,
to where the realm of Good Thought is at one's disposal,
to where the Mindful Lord abides in abundance,

17

so that I may proclaim verses for you,
nothing less than verses, Djāmaaspa son of Hugava,
so that ye have, besides compliance, praises of the Caring One
who discriminates between the just man and the unjust
with His sage adviser Right, He the Mindful Lord.

18

Whoever confers weal on me, on him for my part the best things
at my disposal I confer, with good thought,
but hostilities on him who would subject us to hostility,
so doing justice, Mindful One and Right, to Your preference:
that is how my sapient thought discriminates.

19

Whoever in accord with Right will make real for me,
for Zarathushtra, the utmost splendour of my desiring,
on him — who deserves the world beyond as his reward
with all spiritual acquisitions — (I confer) two milch cows;[13]
of those (other) things Thou, Mindful One, showest Thyself the
    best provider.[14]

---

[13] Or: a milch cow and bull.
[14] 'Those things' are the other-worldly rewards that are beyond Zoroaster's power to
    confer.

YASNA 47

This short poem focuses on the figure of the Bounteous or Liberal Will, which is mentioned in the first line of every stanza.

(1) By following the promptings of the better of the two antithetical Wills and Good Thought, and maintaining goodness in word and deed, one will be rewarded (by the powers above) with life and health. The Lord that we call the Mindful One is mindful indeed of people's merits as he exercises his power, with Piety beside him to identify those who cultivate her.

(2) The influence of the Liberal Will is manifested above all by means of good speech, good actions, and good thinking. In giving definition to these three media Zoroaster works in the names of Good Thought, Piety, Right, and the Mindful One, who is the father of Right.

(3) He is indeed the father of the Liberal Will itself. This Will created, for the man who serves it, the cow (that creature so important in Zoroaster's eyes). This means that she is the product of a good intent that is subordinate to the Mindful One, part of his cosmic plan. He ordained that she should graze in pastures where peace and piety reign, because that man, her herdsman, let himself be guided by Good Thought.

(4) The wrongful divert people from the course indicated by the Liberal Will, both with regard to the cow and otherwise. Not so the righteous: even the poor man who is righteous will be generous to the cause, and even the wealthy one, accustomed to giving to those in greater need, will refuse his largesse to the opponents of the cause.

47.1

On account of bounteous will and best thought
and deed and word in accord with Right
they will give one health and continuing life.
Mindful in his dominion is the Lord with Piety.

2

Of this most Bounteous Will one effects the best (showing)
by utterances with the tongue according to Good Thought,
by Piety's work with the hands,
(and) with this insight: 'He is the father of Right, He the Mindful
    One.'

3

Of this Will Thou art the bounteous father,
(the Will) which fashioned for that (pious) man the gladdening
    cow,
while for her pasture Thou didst establish peace and piety,
because he took counsel, Mindful One, with Good Thought.

4

From this Will, the Bounteous one, the wrongful deflect people,
Mindful One; not so the righteous.
Even the poor man may be kind to the righteous one;
even the man of much means, malign towards the wrongful.

(5) Guided by the Liberal Will, the Mindful Lord has assigned every blessing to those who follow it. Insofar as the wrongful are seen to enjoy good things such as long life and health, it is without his favour, and they will pay for it in the end.

(6) With that same Liberal Will the Lord has ordained that the good and the bad are divided after death by the judgment of fire and each receive their deserts. This confirms and reinforces the validity of Piety and Right; many of those who come to listen to Zoroaster's teaching will be persuaded by the prospect of that post-mortem dispensation.

5

With that Bounteous Will also, Mindful Lord,
Thou didst assign to the righteous one whatever best things there
    be;
it is without Thy favour that the wrongful one partakes of them,
by his own actions abiding on the side of Bad Thought.

6

With that Bounteous Will Thou didst establish, Mindful Lord,
the allocation of the good between the two parties by the fire
that reinforces Piety and Right;
for that will convince many proselytes.

YASNA 48

Apart from the fact that the theme of the Liberal Will is not carried further, this poem might be taken as a continuation of the previous one, with the first line referring back to 47. 6; but it can also refer forwards.

(1) If Right (as embodied in the preachers of Right) succeeds in refuting the claims of the old religion and replacing them with the true gospel that confers continuing life, that will be moral progress, and will add to the credit of the Mindful Lord.

(2) Zoroaster hopes to see this happen in his lifetime, and he would like the Mindful One to assure him that it will be so, that the righteous will triumph over the wrongful, as should be the case in a well-ordered world.

(3) The Mindful Lord's teachings, as mediated to mankind through Zoroaster, are founded on basic laws of the universe that are not all apparent to mankind but are known to him through his supreme sapience. Accordingly they are the best of teachings — provided that one is capable of taking them in.

(4) People fall into two categories according to whether they adopt good thought or bad. They then follow contrasting patterns of speech and behaviour and pursue contrasting aims. The two types of people are all mixed together in this life, but at the last they will be separated and sent different ways.

48.1

Now if thereby Right will vanquish Wrong,
when it *catches up with* the deceitful assertions
by Daevas and mortals in the matter of avoiding death,
then it will increase Thy praise together with Thy strength, Lord.

2

Tell me – Thou art the knowing one, Lord –
before the *end of the course* approaches me:
will the righteous man, Mindful One, vanquish the wrongful?
For that is the pattern of existence found to be good.

3

For him who apprehends it, the best of teachings is
the one that the beneficent Lord teaches with Right,
the bounteous one who knows even hidden laws,
one such as Thou, Mindful One, with the wisdom of Good
Thought.

4

He who sets in place better thought, Mindful One, or worse
follows his moral self in deed and word,
his own pleasures, desires, choices;
(but) in Thy sapience at the last it will go differently.[1]

---

[1] That is, for the adherents of good or bad thought.

(5) May our rulers be of the good kind, endowed with good thought that they put into practice and manifest in their actions. The prayer is addressed to Piety, because she can go to the rulers and attach herself to them.

A complementary element of the good world, besides the purification of humanity, is the breeding and welfare of the cow, which the Mindful Lord has created to provide us with nourishment. (6) It is because of the cow that we enjoy a good way of life and bodily health and vigour, which go hand in hand with good thought. The pastureland with its grass and shrubs are there for her; it is all part of the Mindful Lord's intelligent creation.

(7) So let us have an end to the cruel fury and violence with which the cow's peaceful existence is harassed. That is contrary to good thought and Right, which the well-disposed man adheres to. He dwells in the Mindful One's house.

(8) Zoroaster seeks further reassurance. The Mindful Lord has begun to establish a realm of goodness in part of the earth, but what is the extent of its effectiveness? Has the reward that is due to Zoroaster the power to prevail over the efforts of the wrongful to deprive him of it? Has Right, whose presence in his followers' field of vision is so earnestly desired, the power to inspire them to turn their good intentions into action?

5

Let good rulers rule – do not let bad rulers rule us –
with enactments of good insight, O Piety.
Let purification of breeding, which for man too is best,
be effected for the cow; Thou raisest her for our sustenance.

6

For she it is that gives us easy living, she too vitality
and strength, that pair esteemed of Good Thought,
and for her with Right the Mindful One will have grown the
     plants,
He the Lord at the engendering of the first existence.

7

Let violence be tied down, cut short cruelty,
ye who wish to secure yourselves to Good Thought.
Let it be protected by Right, whose companion the bounteous
     man is;
his lodgings are in Thy house, Lord.

8

What is the potency, Mindful One, of Thy good dominion?
What is that of Thy reward for me, Lord?
What is Thine, O Right, Thou longed-for one in the presence of
     the zealous,
by way of *stimulus* for enactments of the Good Will?

(9) When will he receive confirmation that the Mindful One really has the power to protect him from the dangers that face him? He should be told the whole pattern of the fabric woven by Good Thought. As one of those engaged on the betterment of the world, he would like to know that his reward is guaranteed.

(10) When will the unholy rituals of the old religion, administered by the Karpans in service to the regional rulers, be challenged? Associated with the violence against the cow there is the consumption of the disgusting, intoxicating *haoma* (cf. 32. 14): when will the faithful have the courage to knock it out of the priests' hands?

(11) When will piety and regard for Right prevail in the land, safeguarding the good pastoral way of life? And in which district will the conflict between the two parties be ended, as they all acquire the insight of Good Thought?

(12) Those who do ally themselves with Good Thought and Right, and strive to please the Mindful Lord by acting in accord with his stated law, are the ones who must get rid of 'violence', that is, the traditional cult practice. In this way they will become the reformers and benefactors of the regions.

9

When shall I know it, if Ye have control over something,
Mindful One and Right, whose danger is a threat?
Let me be told straightly Good Thought's *design*;
may the Promoter know how his reward is to be.

10

When, Mindful One, do the men of *Observance* stand ready?
When does one strike out at this liquor piss
with which the Karpans cruelly give one the gripes,
they and the intent misrulers of the regions?

11

When, Mindful One, will Piety together with Right
come in dominion, she of easy pastoral living?
What men will make peace with the bloodthirsty wrongful ones?
To what people will Good Thought's insight come?

12

They will be the Promoters of the regions
who by Good Thought, by actions with Right,
follow what satisfies Thy law, Mindful One;
for they are appointed as the expellers of violence.

YASNA 49

This poem is again concerned with the tension between the followers of the good religion, which Zoroaster hopes to see propagated more widely, and those who serve Wrong.

(1) Zoroaster endeavours to uphold the interests of the pastoralists who cannot defend themselves adequately against aggression, but he has long attracted the enmity and oppression of someone he calls (if the word is rightly translated) the great Polluter – presumably the most prominent of those who corrupt the life of the world with their violence and their animal sacrifices (cf. 32. 10–12, 46. 11). May he be overthrown! The prayer is addressed to Good Dispensation, that is, the power that awards good fortune to people; Zoroaster desires this for himself now.

(2) He is put in mind of that more distant wrongdoer by someone nearer at hand, the spokesman of the traditional religion who gives people false instruction and turns them away from Right. He has failed to embrace true Piety (perhaps treated figuratively as a woman to be taken in marriage), and has not listened to the promptings of Good Thought.

(3) He has Wrong as his designated guide, which will bring him harm, whereas we have Right to look after us on our chosen path. By following it Zoroaster aspires to keep Good Thought ever at his side. He prohibits all adherents of Wrong from accompanying him, in case they deflect him from his goal.

(4) The misguided ones, interlopers in the pastoral society, preach cruel aggression against the cow and, by failing to do what is good, lead others to do what is positively bad. They it is who have established the Daevas as gods of the land, the religion which is that of the wrongful man.

49.1

That greatest *polluter* has fed himself full on my life,[2]
I who seek with Right to do justice to the ill-protected, Mindful
    One.
O Good Dispensation, come to me, support me;
devise his destruction with Good Thought!

2

I am put in mind of this *polluter*
by the wrongful teacher who deceitfully deflects people from
    Right:
he has not embraced bounteous Piety to make her his,
nor, Mindful One, taken counsel with Good Thought.

3

But for this chosen path (of ours), Mindful One, is laid down
Right to strengthen us: for that teacher, Wrong to harm him.
By this path I long for union with Good Thought;
I ban all wrongful ones from my company.

4

Those who in ill wisdom increase violence and cruelty
with their own tongues, non-stockraisers among stockraisers,
through whose failure to do good deeds the ill deeds prevail,
they establish the Daevas, which is the wrongful one's religion.

---

[2] Sense uncertain; some interpret as 'on my grain'.

(5) On the other hand, he whose religious conception is founded on good thought, and on the other good principles of which the Mindful Lord is the patron, is the symbolic counterpart of our bloodless offerings of dairy produce that refreshes and invigorates. Zoroaster makes it clear that he is not referring to a particular individual but to anyone of good family who possesses true piety.

(6) Now, what are the prospects of progress? Let the Mindful One and Right communicate their wisdom, so that Zoroaster and his associates can decide how best to make their religion known.

(7) When people hear the gospel, let them receive it with good thought and in tune with Right; let the Mindful Lord himself listen with them and mark their reactions. Which clan or tribe has he ordained to be the one that will take up the religion and make famous the community in which it originated?

(8) Frashaushtra has set himself on the right road: let the Lord confirm and perfect his happy devotion to Right, and that of Zoroaster himself, who pledges lifelong friendship with Frashaushtra's family.

5

But he, O Mindful One, is the libation and butter offering
who unites his moral self with Good Thought –
any well-born man of piety with Right –
and with all those (virtues) in Thy realm, Lord.

6

I urge You, Mindful One and Right, to speak
with the sapient thought that is Yours,
so we may decide aright how we might broadcast these things,
this religion that is Your follower's, Lord.

7

Let (a man) hear this too, Mindful One, with Good Thought,
let him hear it with Right: listen Thou, Lord.
Which tribe, which clan will it be by (Thy) ordinances
that will give the community a good renown?

8

To Frashaushtra grant that most gladsome union
with Right – this I pray Thee, Mindful Lord –
and to me, (that union) that is in Thy good realm;
we will (all) be dearest friends for ever.

(9) Let us target also the growers of crops, as they fit into Zoroaster's conception of the well-ordered society and are suitable as promoters of it; as a speaker of truth he would not propose an association with anyone unfit. Djāmaaspa and his family have already committed themselves to Right and to competing for the best reward when the time comes to supplicate for it (cf. 30. 2).

(10) That reward they will find in the Mindful Lord's house, where the souls of the righteous are received. There they will find, besides the company of the other souls, the divine essences of the virtues they themselves have cultivated: good thought, reverence (comprising both inner piety and ritual offerings), and more.

(11) The souls of the wrongful, on the other hand, will dwell – literally, and not just figuratively as at present – in the house of Wrong, an unpleasant establishment where only foul food is served.

(12) Zoroaster ends with a renewed appeal to the Mindful One to make it clearer how he is going to help him, his devotee who invokes him with Right and Good Thought and who praises him and prays for his best boons.

9

Let the cultivator hear the teachings, made as he is to be strong —
the straight speaker does not preach union with the wrongful
  one —
since they yoke their moral selves[3] for the best reward
at the Supplication, those Djāmaaspas yoked to Right.

10

And that (reward), Mindful One, Thou dost keep in Thy house:
Good Thought, and the souls of the righteous,
and Reverence, with which are Piety and Libation,
besides . . . that confers lasting dominion.[4]

11

But as for the ill-dominioned, ill-actioned, ill-speaking,
ill-moralled, ill-thinking wrongful ones,
the souls come to them with foul food;
in the house of Wrong they will be veritable lodgers.

12

What hast Thou of help for him who invokes Thee with Right,
for Zarathushtra? What (for him who invokes Thee) with Good
  Thought,
who will propitiate You with praises, Mindful Lord,
praying for that which is the best at Your disposal?

---

3 Like racehorses.
4 The last word (or pair of words) in the line is unintelligible.

YASNA 50

This poem is addressed throughout to the Mindful Lord. Zoroaster presents himself as the Lord's prophet who is singing his praises in 'the house of song' and who hopes for his help in the matter of cattle management.

(1) Zoroaster asks whether his soul, the organ with which he communicates with the higher powers, is at all effective in engaging their support. He needs protection for his holding of livestock and for his own safety, and for this he relies on his trinity, the Mindful Lord, Right, and Good Thought.

(2) How is a righteous man to secure cows for himself when there are so many evil people around, people who bring death to the cow and abhor the righteous living that exists in the light of the sun?[5] May the Lord drive them out and further the rights of the just.

(3) It is only right that the pious man should have the cow of his bad neighbour who lets her be killed for sacrifice. It would increase his social standing. It just requires the intervention of a right-thinking higher authority.

(4) Meanwhile Zoroaster will proclaim before his congregation the praises of the trinity and those of Dominion, the effective authority that would enable him to achieve his ambition.

---

[5] The reference to the sun is not certain, but it fits Zoroaster's thought; cf. stanza 10, and 32. 10.

50.1

Does my soul command any succour?
Who has been found as my cattle's, who as my own protector –
other than Right and Thou, Mindful Lord
reliably invoked, and Best Thought?

2

How, Mindful One, might a man petition for the gladdening cow
if he wished her to be on his pastureland,
a true-living man with Right among the many who *blaspheme* the
    sun?
Drive out those evil ones, adopt the upright one!

3

Yet his, Mindful One, will she rightfully be,
(the cow) that one assigns to him with authority and good thought,
(to) the man who by virtue of the reward would be increased,
that neighbouring creature that the wrongful one has.

4

But I will worship You with praise, Mindful Lord,
together with Right and Best Thought
and that Dominion by which one may stand forth on the path of
    enablement;
facing the zealous I will be heard in the house of song.

(5) After all, it is established in principle that the Mindful Lord and Right will be well disposed towards their 'mantra-man' (*maθran-*), the man who formulates their principles in verse, and will reward him with material assistance – (6) this prophet who is chanting now, their reverent supporter, Zoroaster. May the Lord, with Good Thought, continue to instruct him and guide his eloquence on the path of wisdom.

(7) He by his poetic art will construct the vehicle for them to respond to his invocation and bring him succour; it is pictured, in ancient Indo-Iranian imagery, as a racing chariot drawn by swift, strong, prize-winning horses.

(8) Drawing further on the traditional language of cult hymns, Zoroaster declares how he will worship the Lord with upraised hands beside the fire altar, the central focus of daily worship. Again he emphasizes his piety and reverence and his attachment to Right and Good Thought.

5

For it is established by You, Mindful Lord and Right,
that Ye will favour Your prophet
with conspicuous and visible succour,
with the main force by which one could set us in well-being:

6

this prophet who is bringing forth his voice, Mindful One,
as (Your) ally with Right, in reverence, Zarathushtra.
May He who gives wisdom to hold the reins[6] of my tongue
instruct me in His order with Good Thought.

7

I will yoke You the swiftest steeds,
ones widely victorious, those of Your laudation,
Mindful One and Right, ones sturdy with Good Thought,
with which Ye will win: may Ye be there for my succour.

8

Together with what are known as the Footsteps of Libation[7]
I will approach You, Mindful One, with outstretched hands,
approach You with Right and a zealous man's reverence,
approach You with proficiency in good thought.

---

[6] Literally 'to be the charioteer'.
[7] A traditional phrase, paralleled in the Rigveda, referring to the butter libations splashed on the fire altar.

(9) These whole-hearted acts of worship will be performed, and his good intent translated into action. His priority is to secure his reward from the powers above; after that, to find the means to fulfil his aspirations with the help of a patron on earth.

(10) All his past and future efforts are dedicated to the glorification of the Mindful Lord and Right; all that is beautiful in the world, above all the sunlight that symbolizes pure, well-regulated life, serves him as subject matter for his laudations.

(11) He claims the office of the Mindful Lord's hymnist, and he will discharge it for as long as he can, depending on his having the empowerment that he is now praying for. Will the Lord, who governs the whole of life, join with Good Thought in fulfilling his highest aspirations?

9

With these acts of worship I will come unto You, giving praise,
Mindful One and Right, with enactments of Good Thought.
When I have my reward at my disposal,
then may I find enablement in my benefactor's favour.

10

Whatever things I do, and whatever (I have done) before,
and whatever in accord with good thought has a claim on the
    eyes,
the light of the sun, the *potent* Ox of Days,[8]
are for Your lauding with Right, Mindful Lord.

11

I will declare myself Your praise-singer, Mindful One, and will
    be so,
as long as I have the strength and ability with Right.
Will the Ordainer of the World carry through with Good
    Thought
the realization of the utmost splendour of my desiring?

---

[8] Cf. 46. 3 with note.

YASNA 51

This carefully articulated composition is one of the most substantial in the collection; only *Yasna* 31 has as many stanzas, though other poems are longer by line-count. It may be divided into five segments: (1–3) prefatory; (4–11) presentation of Zoroaster's anxieties, appeal for support, antithesis of righteous and unrighteous; (12–14) denunciation of unrighteous individuals; (15–20) praise of righteous ones; (21–2) closing affirmations.

(1) Zoroaster begins with remarks on the importance of good *xšaθra-*, authority or control that gives one freedom of action in a given area. It brings notable benefits – not least to the patron of a religious ceremony at which dairy produce is offered. (This must be an allusion to the occasion; cf. stanzas 15–16.) For it to 'travel across' between heaven and earth, linking divine principle and earthly reality, the best medium is its righteous exercise in actual situations. Such mediation between heaven and earth was a traditional Indo-Iranian concept in the context of a religious ceremony; in the Rigveda it may be performed by the sacred fire or by the poet's hymn, and so here Zoroaster is going to mediate with his hymn for those present.

(2) The authority that he himself exercises is over the art of poetic composition, and this he will display in what follows, addressing first the Mindful Lord, Right, and Piety. He prays that they will exercise the authority that they have of strengthening or enhancement to the advantage of (or in return for) his song of praise.

(3) Let them turn their ears toward those who are siding with them by thought, word, and deed, and who have taken the Mindful Lord as their number one teacher.

51.1

Good authority is the thing to choose, most productive of fortune,
certainly for one liberal with libation. It descends best
through actions with Right, Mindful One, and this I will put into
  practice for us here and now.

2

So first I will show to You, Mindful Lord, and to Right
and to Thee, Piety, the authority at my command:
Yours of enhancement apply Thou with Good Thought to my
  laudation.

3

Let Your ears focus on those who by their actions are uniting
  with You,
O Lord and Right, and by their tongue's utterances of good
  thought,
those of whom Thou, Mindful One, art the first teacher.

(4) After this introduction we come to the substance. The situation is far from good. There is much misery and cruelty; right, piety, and good thought are not much in evidence. The Mindful Lord does not seem to be in command of those areas where he ought to be.

(5) To be more specific, the honest herdsman has not got complete control of the cattle, as he should have according to Right. This despite his prudence and piety: faced with the moral choice that will determine whether he is rewarded or punished, he correctly discerns that the righteous will get their just deserts.

(6) If someone makes the best choices and is zealous in following the Lord's preferences, he takes note of him and, in exercising his power over his fate hereafter, gives him his just reward; but anyone who fails to serve him suffers grievously for it at the end of the course.

(7) It was the Mindful One who made the cow and those features of the natural world that provide her and us with nourishment, the waters and the plants. May he sustain them and preserve Zoroaster from sickness and death, debility, lassitude, and bad thought, so that he can go on preaching the word.

4

Where does *respect* appear instead of harm, where mercy?
Where lustre-giving Right? Where bounteous Piety?
Where Best Thought? Where Thy areas of control, Mindful One?

5

All this I ask: how in accord with Right the cow is acquired
by the herdsman upright in his actions, prudent, reverent,
one who, with the two rewards at his disposal, discerns aright
    the ruling made for the just.

6

If one is choosing what is better than good, and if one will be
    prompt to His will,
the Lord is mindful in His dominion; but it is worse than bad for
    him
that will not serve Him, at the last bend of worldly life.[1]

7

Grant me, Thou who didst fashion the cow and the waters and
    plants,
continuing life and health through Thy most bounteous will,
    Mindful One,
strength and vitality with good thought in my teaching.

---

[1] Cf. 43. 5 with note.

(8–9) Continuing to address the Mindful Lord, Zoroaster repeats the message of stanza 6. (The Lord, he acknowledges, does not need to be told it; there is nothing a man knows that he does not. So Zoroaster can speak without fear of disagreement.) The message is that the follower of Wrong pays dearly for it, whereas he who has embraced Right gets what he would wish, in that judgment by fire and molten metal which identifies the bad people and condemns them to their wretched fate.

(10) If Zoroaster were to suffer in consequence of that, it would be because he deserved it, and he could not complain. But anyone who attacks him otherwise is a wrongdoer. For his part he expects the good reward, and he calls upon Right to bring it to him.

(11) Let us review individual cases. Who is on Zoroaster's side and who is not? Who, in his mental deliberations, has consulted with Right and Piety? Which upright man has taken thought for the *maga-*, the great religious event that Zoroaster mentions several times elsewhere?

8

For I will tell Thee, Mindful One — of course a man can only say
    what Thou knowest —
that amid ill for the wrongful one, but in bliss for him who has
    embraced Right
(happy that prophet who speaks to one who knows!)

9

is the atonement that Thou didst set for the two parties through
    Thy flaming fire, Mindful One,
and through molten metal, to establish proof about our characters
for the harm of the wrongful one and the strengthening of the
    righteous.

10

The man who harms me otherwise than that, Mindful One,
is a son of the Creator of Wrong, and thus a malefactor (of all)
    who are:
for myself I will call upon Right to come with the good reward.

11

What man is ally to Spitāma Zarathushtra, Mindful One?
Or who has taken counsel with Right? With whom is bounteous
    Piety?
Or what upright man has gained the insight for Good Thought's
    rite?

(12) To begin with the bad people: the Kavi and Karpan priests come to mind (cf. 32. 12–15, 44. 20, 46. 11). As for the Kavis, not all of them are bad (cf. stanza 16), but Zoroaster can point to a servant of a Kavi or of Kavis who has shown him hostility.

(13) That episode of a difficult crossing illustrates how those with a false value system disregard the truth recognized by the upright. When that wrongdoer dies and comes to another crossing, the Arbiter's, and meets his own soul standing there on the path of Wrong because of the things he has said and done, then he will be sorry.

(14) The Karpans likewise have sinned in word and deed, promoting and practising cruelty to the cow. They too will ultimately be condemned to follow the path that leads to the House of Wrong.

(15) Now Zoroaster turns to those who merit praise. This is the reward that the poet can confer, the one that he says he has promised earlier to those who undertook to hold the ceremony and provide the offerings.[2] (Perhaps he is recalling stanza 1, where he held out the prospect of 'fortune' for the patron of such an event as this.) The Mindful Lord, of course, must precede them in the sequence of those to be praised in the song; under the guidance of Good Thought, Zoroaster has vowed to praise him and Right for the benefits they confer.

---

[2] This parallels the relationship seen between the Vedic Rishi and the wealthy patron of the sacrifice.

12

He was not pleased with the Kavi catamite at the crossing in the
winter,
(he,) Zarathushtra Spitāma, when the emissary had barred his
way at it,
when those two draught animals of his were trembling from the
journey and the cold.

13

So the wrongful one's morality may ignore the just one's reality;
(but) his soul will torment him at the Arbiter's Crossing when it
confronts him,
lost through his own actions and his tongue's from the path of
Right.

14

The Karpans are not fit allies from the standpoint of (Your)
ordinances and the pasture,
manifesters of harm to the cow by their actions and proclamations –
proclamation that will consign them at the last to the house of
Wrong.

15

As for the reward that Zarathushtra earlier assigned to the patrons
of the rite,
the Mindful Lord enters the house of song first:
so it was assigned to You together with Good Thought, and to
Right, because of (Your) power to strengthen.

(16) Vishtaaspa, the principal patron, has followed Good Thought, meditated on Right, and arrived at the insight, 'Bounteous is the Mindful Lord', which he now proclaims to others to the Zoroastrians' satisfaction.

(17) Frashaushtra, as elsewhere (46. 16, 49. 8), appears as someone dear to Zoroaster and interested in his religion – he 'exposes his body' to it, as one might to the sun – but not yet fully committed to it. May the Lord, who has the power to do so, make him an enthusiast, so that Right will look on him with favour.

(18) His brother Djāmaaspa is already converted. He has opted for the religion's insight and the province in which Good Thought holds sway. May the Mindful One give him his support.

(19) Madyaimāha, a member of the prophet's own Spitāma family, gets an honourable mention, but nothing positive is actually said of his piety. He is told that the support of the Mindful Lord referred to in the previous stanza is sought through religion. One must pronounce the Lord's ordinances, and better still live in accord with them; that is the way to win a life.

16

That insight the Kavi Vishtaaspa, with his control of the rite, attained
by the paths of Good Thought, the one which he meditated with Right,
to proclaim for us as we desired, 'Bounteous is the Mindful Lord'.

17

Frashaushtra son of Hugava exposes his person that I esteem
to the Good Religion; let it be made desirable to him
by the one who has the power, the Mindful Lord, for his attaining Right's favour.

18

That insight Djāmaaspa son of Hugava, illustrious in his competence,
chooses to find with Right, that realm of Good Thought.
Grant him, Mindful Lord, that of Thine which gives support.

19

The man, O Madyaimāha Spitāma, gets that (support) for himself,
apprehending it with his moral self, who, petitioning for worldly life,
speaks the Mindful One's ordinances, (and gets it) all the better
because of his lifetime conduct.

(20) Zoroaster sums up with a collective address to his followers. The benefit he has described is available to all of them who agree in worshipping Right with good thought, good speech, piety, and reverence of the Mindful Lord.

(21) One's moral and religious outlook and positive thought, speech, and conduct are in one's own control. For further blessings such as (righteous) prosperity and (wisely exercised) authority we depend on the Lord, and Zoroaster prays to him for them.

(22) In conclusion he affirms his faith that the worship of the Mindful One is his best course. He rejects the traditional religion with its pantheon of named deities: the immortal powers who are for ever he will call by their real names, Good Thought, the Bounteous Will, Piety, and so forth, and attend them with devotion.

20

This strengthening is ours to give you, all ye of one mind
who worship Right with good thought and utterance – and with
    you is Piety –
in reverence of the Mindful One who affords succour.

21

The man of Piety, he is bounteous in insight, words, conduct,
morality. Right with prosperity, authority with good thought,
the Mindful Lord bestows: to Him I pray for the good reward.

22

I know in whose worship in accord with Right is my best
    (interest):
the Mindful Lord.[3] Those (immortals) who have been and are
I will worship under their own names, and attend them with
    devotion.

---

3 Or 'The Mindful Lord knows in whose' etc. The verse was so construed, apparently,
by the author of 27. 15; see above, p. 23.

YASNA 53 + 54.1

This poem has a more elaborate metrical structure than any other in the collection. Certain linguistic details, and the way in which Zoroaster is referred to, suggest that it is not by him; he is revered as a patriarch, one perhaps no longer among the living. The occasion is apparently the wedding of one Porucistā, described as a daughter of Zoroaster, though we cannot be sure whether this is to be taken literally or as a term for a female follower and adherent.

(1) Zoroaster's reputation has become established and the virtue of his religion acknowledged, if it is accepted that he, and all who mould their speech and behaviour to his teaching, have won or will win the life of continual bliss from the Mindful Lord.

(2) Let his followers therefore set themselves to please the Mindful One by their thoughts, words, and deeds, to worship and praise him, and not to go astray from the path of this religion that he has given us.

Notable among the followers, and deserving mention by name (as in several other poems), are the Kavi Vishtaaspa and Frashaushtra. Vishtaaspa is now given the surname Spitāma and called *Zaraϑuštriš*, literally Zoroaster's son – surely not something he had always been, but something he had become by marriage or adoption, or just honorifically as disciple.[1] Was he the bridegroom, who is not otherwise identified?

(3) The bride is now addressed. She is of the Haecataspa Spitāmas, a branch of the family that Zoroaster addresses at 46. 15, but at the same time she is called Zoroaster's daughter; again this could be an honorific designation. She is exhorted to attend unremittingly to Good Thought, as that will link her directly with the other two members of the trinity, Right and the Mindful Lord

---

[1] Cf. the expression in 54. 1 below, 'the men and women of Zarathushtra'.

53. 1

Supreme in renown is the capability of Zarathushtra
Spitāma, if (it is true that) in accord with Right
the Mindful Lord will grant him blessings for ever, the good
　existence,
and to those who *practise* and master his Good Religion's speech
　and conduct.

2

So let them accord in thought, speech, and conduct
in what gratifies the Mindful One, with devotion to His praise,
　and acts of worship —
the Kavi Vishtaaspa too, the Spitāma Zoroastrian, and Frasha-
　ushtra —
the straight paths of the gift the Lord gives, the religion of the
　Promoter.

3

Be resolute, Porucistā of the Haecataspa Spitāmas,
youngest of Zarathushtra's daughters,
in attendance to Good Thought: it gives thee union with Right
　and the Mindful One.
So take counsel with thy reason; perform piety's most liberal
　benefactions.

himself. She should let good sense govern her conduct, and do the good works that proceed from piety.

(4) The admonitions are now directed more generally to young people approaching marriage. The married woman (the wife of a stock-raiser is envisaged) should devotedly minister to all the menfolk's needs: her husband's, her father's, those of the dependent herdsmen, and those of other clansmen. Marriage is part of the Mindful Lord's plan; its benefits, the product of Good Thought, accrue lifelong to those who uphold his religion.

(5) The poet has advice not only for girls getting married but also for their bridegrooms, who should commit themselves to the life guided by Good Thought: this should be their governing principle, both for themselves and for their wives. They should compete with each other in their attachment to Right – it will be to their advantage.

(6) Such is the advice for the separate sexes. Now it becomes more universal. But the next lines do not give coherent meaning, and contain far too many words for a single stanza; clearly two stanzas have become conflated, with the loss of parts of both. The sense may have been, 'when you see the wrongful one apparently prospering, it is only temporary, for he will certainly come to a bad end.' (6a) The second stanza contained further description of the bad ones' fate. They will be consigned to the House of Wrong, with only foul food to eat. Do not associate or co-operate with such people, or you will be assisting in the corruption of the spiritual world.

4

For I will *urge on* you (girls) the zeal with which one should serve
    her father
and husband, herdsmen, and clan too,
a righteous one (serving) the righteous; the sunny fruits of Good
    Thought, *cognisant of marriage ties,*
the Mindful Lord bestows on the Good Religion for ever.

5

I speak precepts for girls marrying
and for you, bridegrooms: take them to heart.
Be acquiring by your moralities, for your brides too, the life of
    Good Thought;
let one among you vie with another in right, for that will profit
    him.

6

These truths are like this, gentlemen; like so, ladies.
Of him that is attached to Wrong, the prosperity ye see
*   *   *   *   *   *   *   *
*   *   of Wrong: I take away his defences from his body.

6a

*   *   *   *   *   *
*   *   *   *   *   *
*   *   foul food for them as they cry 'Woe'; well-being
    is lost
for the wrongful diminishers of Right. With them ye ruin spiritual
    life.

(7) The present ceremony comes back into focus.[2] Marriage, conducted according to the proper procedure, offers men a desirable prize. The bridegroom will be able to consummate the union confident of his bride's virginity. The wrongful one may have lusted after her, but she has remained pure. If the institution of marriage is set aside, however, the consequences will be disastrous.

(8) Let this ceremony therefore frustrate the wicked and make them objects of derision. (The execration now becomes more general:) May we have good rulers who will beat, injure, kill them, leaving our settlements to enjoy their peaceful pastoral life. And may this come about soon.

(9) Because of those who opt for Wrong, corruption of the world sets in. They are bent on diminishing Right and oppressing good people. But they are condemned to perdition. We are just waiting for the righteous ruler who can put a stop to their activities and eliminate them. That lies in the Mindful Lord's power to arrange; with that power he could improve the lot of the virtuous poor.

---

[2] Or so it seems to us. It is possible that the lost parts of the preceding lines contained something relevant, for example a condemnation of extra-marital sex.

7

But there will be a reward for you from this ceremony:
one will apply his member in fullest confidence under (his bride's)
thighs,
dipping onward and down, where the wrongful one's intent was
frustrated before.
Reject this ceremony, and 'Woe' will be your ultimate word.

8

Hereby let the evildoers be thwarted
and mocked, all of them; let them wail,
by good rulers let them be beaten and bloodied, and let peace be
thereby established for the manorial settlements;
let there come upon them that greatest woe with the fetter of
death; and let it be soon!

9

Through those who make ill choice, decay takes hold: they are
waning and darkness, [3]
those eager diminishers of Right, their persons are forfeit.
Where is the righteous lord who could deprive them of their life
and freedom?
That power, Mindful One, is Thine, whereby to the right-living
poor man Thou canst grant the better lot.

---

[3] Text and sense uncertain.

(54. 1) May Aryaman, the traditional Indo-Iranian personifi-
cation of community ties, including those of marriage, confer his
blessing on the Zoroastrian congregation, strengthening the reli-
gion with social cohesion. May the poet himself win the reward
that the Mindful Lord established for Right.

54.1[4]

Let Aryaman, the one longed for, come to support
the men and women of Zarathushtra,
to support Good Thought, through which the moral self may win
   desirable recompense.
I pray for Right's reward, the longed-for one that the Mindful
   Lord conceives.

---

[4] This stanza is transmitted as the first section of chapter 54 of the *Yasna*, and also as
chapter 27. 5, so not as part of the *Gāthās* proper. But in its very distinctive metrical
form and its Old Avestan language it belongs with *Yasna* 53, and it may have formed
part of the wedding poem from the beginning; the old Indo-Iranian god Aryaman
invoked in it was associated with social and marital ties. It was not necessarily the last
stanza of the poem: it would go as well at the beginning. The prayer took on a life of
its own, being regarded as a general defence against illness, magic, and evil (*Yasna* 54.
2, *Yasht* 3. 5, *Gāh* 1. 6, *Vīdēvdāt* 20. 12, cf. 22. 6–20), and it has traditionally been
used in the Zoroastrian marriage ritual. That is no doubt the reason why it is separated
off from *Yasna* 53 in the Avestan canon.

The Liturgy in Seven Chapters
(Yasna Haptaŋhāiti)

I

Yasna 35

2   We are they who approve of good thoughts, good words, good deeds, here and elsewhere, present and past: we are not revilers of what is good.

3   This we have chosen, Mindful Lord, with Right the comely, to think and speak and do those things that may be the best actions in the world, for both existences.[1]

4   For the cow hereby, with these actions that are the best, we urge the maintenance of peace and pasture, on them that hear and them that hear not, on them that have authority and them that have not authority.

5   To the best ruler we dedicate, assign, and inaugurate rule, so far as lies with us; that is, to the Mindful Lord and to best Right.

6   As anyone, man or woman, knows a truth, so, it being good, let him then both put it into effect for himself and communicate it to those who will put it into effect just as it is.

7   But it is the Mindful Lord's worship and praise that we have apprehended as the greatest good, and the cow's pasture. This we will put into effect for You and communicate so far as we are able.

8   It is in union with Right, in the community of Right, that I declare the best aspiration to lie for anyone in the world, for both existences.

9/10 These words that we speak, Mindful Lord, we will proclaim with better thought of Right. We make Thee both their recipient and their teacher, (10) in accord with Right

---

[1] The material and the spiritual.

and Good Thought and Good Rule, be it with praises where praises are due or with utterances where utterance or with act of worship where acts of worship.

II

Yasna 36

1   With this Fire's community firstly we attend Thee, Mindful Lord, Thee with Thy most Bounteous Will, (the fire) which is torment for him whom Thou puttest to torment.

2   As the most joyous one mayest Thou come for our supplicating, O Fire of the Mindful Lord; with the most joyous one's joy, with the most reverent one's reverence mayest Thou come for our greatest of supplications.

3   Yea, the Fire of the Mindful Lord art Thou; yea, His most Bounteous Will art Thou; or whatever is Thy most *preferred* name, O Fire of the Mindful Lord, with that we attend Thee.

4/5 With Good Thought, with good Right, with good Insight's deeds and words we attend Thee, (5) we revere Thee, we give Thee thanks, Mindful Lord: with all good thoughts, with all good words, with all good deeds we attend Thee.

6   Fairest body of Thy bodies we proclaim this daylight, Mindful Lord; highest of the high yonder sun since it was named.

III

Yasna 37

1/3 In this fashion we worship the Mindful Lord, who created the cow and Right; and the Waters He created, and the good plants, and the light he created, and the earth, and all things good, (2) through His dominion and greatness and artistries.

Him we worship with the prime rites of worship (of them) that dwell in accord with the cow; (3) Him we worship in the names of Lord, Wisdom-choosing, Most Bounteous; Him we worship with our bodily frames and energies; Him we worship in the commitments[2] of the followers of Right, both men and women.

4   Best Right we worship as the fairest, as bounteous, as immortal, as daylit, as encompassing every good;

5   and Good Thought we worship, and good Dominion, and good Morality, and good *Respect*, and good Piety.

IV

Yasna 38

1 / 2   This Earth together with its Dames[3] we worship: her that carries us, and them that are Thy Dames, Mindful Lord, that are desirable in accord with Right, these we worship: — (2) the Libations, the Purifications, the Consummations, the Pieties. With them, good Reward, good Vigour, good Oblation, good Laudation, good Abundance we worship.

3   The Waters we worship, sparkling and sappy, the Lord's Wives that speed on by the Lord's artistry. You of good fording, of good current, of good bathing-pools we present for both existences.[4]

---

[2] That is, the commitment each has made by choosing the good religion. The word rendered 'commitment', *fravaši-*, later came to mean the personal soul that existed before birth and after death.

[3] The term apparently reflects a traditional concept of terrestrial goddesses or nymphs. The Zoroastrian has given them new identities as personifications of religious offices.

[4] This may refer to libations of water.

4   Thus with the names that the Mindful Lord gave you, O Good Ones, when that maker of good made you, with them we worship you, with them we propitiate, with them we reverence, with them we give thanks.

5   As the Waters, as the Milch Cows, as the Mothers, choice cows, caring for the needy, giving to all to drink, we will invoke you, best ones, fairest ones. I will assist you, Good Ones, with the long arm of my liberality at your arrivings, O distributors, personable ones, mothers full of life.

V

Yasna 39

1 / 2   In this fashion we worship the Cow's Soul and her Maker; and our own souls, and those of the livestock that seek our favour – those for whom they exist and those who exist for them – (2) and the souls of the wild creatures that are harmless we worship. And the souls of the followers of Right we worship, wherever born, both men's and women's, those whose better selves prevail or will prevail or have prevailed.

3   And in this fashion we worship the Good Ones male and female, the bounteous, the immortal, the ever-living, the ever-blessing, (the males) that dwell on the side of Good Thought, and the females likewise.

4   As Thou, Mindful Lord, dost conceive and utter and institute and do those things that are good, so we dedicate them to Thee, so we assign them; so hereby we worship Thee, so we reverence, so we give thanks to Thee, Mindful Lord.

5   With a good clan's clanship we attend Thee, that of good Right, of good *Respect*, of good Piety.

VI

Yasna 40

1 / 2 At these oblations, Mindful Lord, exercise Thy mindfulness and Thy abundance: our offering will *justify* it,[5] so far as lies with us. The . . .[6] reward which Thou hast appointed for (good) moral selves, Mindful Lord, (2) grant us of it both for this existence and for the spiritual one, that of it by which we might attain that (prize), association with Thee and with Right for evermore.

3 Grant us men, Mindful Lord, right-doers and right-seekers, peaceful herdsmen, for enduring, nourishing, solid association with us and support by us.

4 So may it be with the clan, so with the communities, so with the societies we associate with; so also may it be with us for You, Mindful Lord, us upright followers of Right, as we offer *what we are able*.

VII

Yasna 41

1 Praises, songs, laudations for the Mindful Lord and best Right we dedicate and assign and proclaim.

2 Thy good dominion, Mindful Lord, may we attain for evermore: may a good ruler, whether man or woman, assume rule over us in both existences, O most beneficent of beings.

3 Thee the blessed, the nourishing, the worshipful, the adherent of Right, we adopt: so mayest Thou be our life and substance in both existences, O most beneficent of beings.

---

[5] Literally 'with (our) offering it will *befit* Thee'.
[6] Unintelligible adjective.

4   May we earn and may we win, Mindful Lord, Thy long-
     lasting support, and may we become potent and strong
     through Thee, and mayest Thou long support us and in the
     way we desire, O most beneficent of beings.

5/6   We declare ourselves Thy praisers and prophets, Mindful
     Lord, and we stand willing and ready. The . . . reward
     which Thou hast appointed for (good) moral selves, Mind-
     ful Lord, (6) grant us of it both for this existence and for
     the spiritual one, that of it by which we may attain that
     (prize), union with Thee and with Right for evermore.

Notes on the Text

To whom it may concern: I give here a list of variant readings I have chosen to adopt. Those marked with an asterisk are conjectural emendations by myself; I have argued for most of them in *Iran* 45 (2008), 126–33.

The Gāthās

29. 8b *mazdå*. See *Iran* 44 (2007), 81 f.
30. 7c Deleting *aiiaŋhā* with Kuiper.
30. 11a **saśaϑā* (subjunctive).
31. 8c Read perhaps **hiϑāum*.
31. 21a **sarō<i>*.
32. 1c Reading *daraiiō* with Humbach.
32. 8b Reading *gōuš* with Andreas and Wackernagel.
32. 14c **haoməm* for *auuō*.
32. 16c **åŋhaiiā* (causal of *āh-*, subjunctive with disyllabic *-ā*).
33. 9a **ašā uxšaiiaṇtəm*.
33. 10a **vīspås tå*.
33. 13a **ā bifrā*.
34. 5 **hiiaṯ ā vō ahmī*.
34. 8ab Reading *biiaiṇtī* with ms. J2 and *aš.aojå* with Insler.
34. 10c **xšaϑrōi yā*.
34. 11b Reading *xraϑβā* with ms. K5.
43. 9d Reading *ādā* after ms. J2 (*aδā*; *adā* Insler).
43. 10d **išəṇtąm* for *ōmauuaṇtąm*.

43. 16d *xšaϑrā.
44. 9c *tąm for yąm.
44. 10e *ϑβōi.
44. 12c *aiiōm vā for aŋgrō vā.
44. 17b *Deleting Mazdā to restore the metre.
44. 19d, e Reading ąsaṯ . . . ąsaṯ with Schwyzer.
45. 3b Reading yā with ms. J6.
46. 5a *ā dąm.
46. 14c Analysing yāhī with Insler as yā ahī.
46. 17c *və stōi.
47. 4b ašauuanō.
48. 1b *ąsaṯ tā.
48. 2b Reading yāmə̄ṇg as one word with Insler.
50. 2d Reading with Insler akąs tə̄ṇg mā niš ąsiiā.
50. 7d Reading yāiš ā zāϑā.
51. 3b *Ahurā.
51. 5a *pərəsā.
51. 12c Reading with Insler ī for īm, which appears to have come in from verse a.
51. 18c *hōi.
51. 19c *mrauuaṯ.
53. 3a Following Insler's reading (tə̄ṇcā) and interpretation.
53. 4a *spərədəm. But varānī remains unexplained.
53. 5b Reading vadəmnā with Insler, or *vadəmnåŋhō for better metre.
53. 8c Reading and parsing as Kellens–Pirart.
53. 9a Reading rajīš (mss. V Mf1) and following Humbach's interpretation.

The Seven Chapters

35. 7 *Omitting the first və.
35. 10 *Omitting Ahurā after the first ϑβaṯ, which must have been mistaken for the pronoun 'thee'.
37. 4 *<hiiaṯ> aməšəm.
40. 4 Reading xᵛaētuš with eight mss. and ərəšuuā with two.

Bibliography

Translations and commentaries

The principal modern scholarly translations of the *Gāthās* are:

Lommel, Herman, *Die Gathas des Zarathustra*, Basel–Stuttgart 1971. (German translation, notes.)

Insler, Stanley, *The Gāthās of Zarathustra*, Teheran–Leiden 1975 (*Acta Iranica*, 8). (Text, translation, commentary.)

Kellens, Jean, and Eric Pirart, *Les textes vieil-avestiques*, 3 vols., Wiesbaden 1988–90. (Text, French translation, philological essays and notes.)

Humbach, Helmut, *The Gāthās of Zarathushtra*, 2 vols., Heidelberg 1991. (Introduction, text, translation, commentary.)

———, and P. Ichaporia, *The Heritage of Zarathushtra. A New Translation of his* Gāthās, Heidelberg 1994.

A translation widely used and respected among Zoroastrians is that by Piloo Nanavutty, *The Gathas of Zarathustra* (Ahmedabad 1999).

Kellens–Pirart and Humbach include the *Seven Chapters*, for which one must also use the detailed editions by Johanna Narten, *Der Yasna Haptaŋhāiti* (Wiesbaden 1986) and Almut Hintze, *A Zoroastrian Liturgy. The Worship in Seven Chapters (Yasna 35–41)* (Wiesbaden 2007).

General works

Boyce, Mary, *Zoroastrians. Their Religious Beliefs and Practices*, London 1979.

———, *Textual Sources for the Study of Zoroastrianism*, Manchester 1984.

———, *A History of Zoroastrianism*, i–iii, Leiden–Köln 1975–91.

Clark, Peter, *Zoroastrianism. An Introduction to an Ancient Faith*, Brighton 1998.

Duchesne-Guillemin, Jacques, *The Western Response to Zoroaster*, Oxford 1958.

———, *La religion de l'Iran ancien*, Paris 1962; trans. K. M. Jamasp Asa as *Religion of Ancient Iran*, Bombay 1973.

Frye, R. N., *The Heritage of Persia*, 2nd ed., London 1976.

Gnoli, Gherardo, *Zoroaster's Time and Homeland*, Naples 1980.

Godrej, Pheroza J. and Firoza P. Mistree (eds.), *A Zoroastrian Tapestry. Art, Religion, and Culture*, Ahmedabad–Middletown N.J. 2002.

Jackson, A. V. Williams, *Zoroaster. The Prophet of Ancient Iran*, New York 1898.

Kellens, Jean, *Essays on Zarathustra and Zoroastrianism*, Costa Mesa, Cal. 2000.

Malandra, William W., *An Introduction to Ancient Iranian Religion. Readings from the Avesta and Achaemenid Inscriptions*, Minneapolis 1983.

Modi, J. J., *The Religious Ceremonies and Customs of the Parsees*, 2nd ed., Bombay 1937.

Moulton, J. H., *Early Zoroastrianism*, London 1913.

Schwartz, Martin, 'The Religion of Achaemenian Iran', in *The Cambridge History of Iran*, ii, Cambridge 1985, 664–97.

Stausberg, Michael, *Die Religion Zarathushtras. Geschichte – Gegenwart – Rituale*, 3 vols., Stuttgart 2002–4.

———, *Zarathustra und seine Religion*, Munich 2005.

——— and Yuhan S.-D. Vevaina (eds.), *Blackwell's Companion to the Study of Zoroastrianism*, in preparation.

Zaehner, R. C., *The Dawn and Twilight of Zoroastranism*, London 1961; repr. London 2002.